Gaelic Names for Celtic Dogs

John A. K. Donovan

Edited by:
William W. Denlinger and R. Annabel Rathman

Alpine
PUBLICATIONS
Loveland, CO 80537

Terra cotta plaque of a Scottish Deerhound, by Augustus Saint Gaudens, N.A., 1884, now in The Smithsonian Institution. *Photo courtesy of the Smithsonian Institution.*

Copyright 1995 Alpine Publications, Inc.,
Copyright 1980 William W. Denlinger

Library of Congress Cataloging-in-Publication Data

Donovan, John A. K.
   Gaelic names for Celtic dogs / by John A.K. Donovan ; edited by William W. Denlinger and R. Annabel Rathman.
      p.   cm.
   Previously published : Fairfax, Va. : Denlinger's, c1980.
   Includes bibliographical references.
   ISBN 0-931866-86-3
   1. Dogs--Names.   2. Names, Gaelic.   3. Dogs--Ireland--History.
4. Dogs--Scotland--History.   I. Denlinger, William Watson, 1924-
II. Rathman, R. Annabel.   III. Title.
SF422.3.D66 1995
929.9'7--dc20   95-39371
                                              CIP

This book is available at special quantity discounts for breeders and for club promotions, premiums, or educational use. Write for details.

Cover design by Betty Jo McKinney

Printed in the United States of America.

Foreword

The early races of Scotia, as Ireland was first called, and of Alban, as Scotland was known in ancient times, were all of Celtic origin. The Celts, who were originally one of the Indo-European peoples, came from the East by several routes. Perhaps the best-known route is that of the first group of Celts, the Milesians, who came through Spain from Scythia, a region in southeastern Europe and Asia. The Firbolgs and the Fomorians, who also were of Celtic stock, probably came from Greece. These three combined Celtic races are the ancestors of the Irish, the Manx, and the Scottish Highlanders. They brought with them the Gaelic language. They also brought with them the dogs, mostly of Greyhound and Terrier types, which were the progenitors of the dogs considered native to Ireland and Scotland today.

In addition to these three branches of the Celtic race—the Milesians, the Firbolgs, and the Fomorians—there were said to be the Tuatha De Danann or "Peoples of the Goddess Danu," who were supposed to have great proficiency in all things magic. Their actual existence is doubtful, but the legends relating to them point up the importance of the female in Celtic society, for the matriarchal nature of Celtic civilization is also a focal point of ancient and medieval history.

In the great Gaelic epic *Tain Bo Cuailgne*, the two principal characters are Queen Medb (pronounced Maeve) and Cuchulain (or Cu Cullan). The title of the epic is translated "The Odyssey of the Cuailgne Bull," and a modern translation of the text into English has been accomplished by the poet Thomas Kinsella.

Anyone writing about Celtic history or legend, especially anyone concerned with the importance of the dog, must stress the odyssey of Cuchulain, who was the greatest of all legendary Celtic heroes, and whose fiercest opponent was Queen Medb. The two were always locked in mortal combat over the possession of cattle and dogs, so in this work we treat Cuchulain as the patron of the Celtic dogs and Queen Medb as their patroness.

Cuchulain's Tain, or odyssey, took place during the time when Conor Mac Nessa was King of the Province of Ulster. Warlike days were those, when the Red Branch Knights of Emania marched as the most glorious of all warriors. Cuchulain as a youth had the ambition to join the Red Branch Knights, so he traveled to Emania. Upon his arrival, he met some local youths playing on the field, and so great was his prowess even then that he easily bested all the other contestants. His reputation grew rapidly and impressively, so he soon was admitted into the Red Branch Knights.

According to the Tain, Queen Medb was the daughter of the *Ard Rhi*, or High King of all Ireland, and was initially married to Conor Mac Nessa, King of Ulster. They separated, and through her second husband, Medb became the Queen of the Kingdom of Connaught. Then, having other worlds to conquer, she was married to Ailill, King of the Kingdom of Leinster. Not being a retiring personality, Medb wanted the size and quality of her posessions to be greater than those of Ailill.

In their rivalry over ownership of dogs and cattle, Medb and Ailill fell out over Ailill's ownership of a great bull which was said to be of unmatched quality except for "The Brown Bull of Cuailgne," a town in the Kingdom of Ulster. In her effort to best Ailill, Queen Medb invited the Chieftain of Cuailgne to bring his bull to her court. He did so, but during a banquet honoring the bull, a great controversy arose and the Chieftain went home with his bull.

Incensed and disappointed, Queen Medb organized a great force and invaded the Kingdom of Ulster in pursuit of the bull. She coaxed the Chieftain successfully at first, but eventually he objected to letting her have the bull, so Queen Medb started an all-out war in which she attacked Ulster aided by a force under Fergus MacRigh, a cousin and enemy of Ulster's King Conor Mac Nessa. With the support of Conor Mac Nessa, who as her former husband resented Queen Medb, Cuchulain placed himself in the Gap of Ulster and all by himself repulsed the armies of four-fifths of Ireland led by Queen Medb. Thus, The Brown Bull of Cuailgne was saved by the hero, Cuchulain.

This episode ended with a great duel between Cuchulain and his close friend Ferdiad, which continued for four days. At the end of each of the first three days, the two would embrace each other, but on the fourth day, Cuchulain ended the career of Ferdiad as described in a translation of the Tain by O'Curry:

"That is enough now, surely," said Ferdiad.
"I fall of that. But I may say, surely,
that I am sickly now after thee. And it
did not behove thee that I should fall by thy hand."
Cuchulain ran toward him after that
and clasped his arms around him, and
lifted him with his arms and his armour,
Cuchulain laid Ferdiad down then; and a trance
and a faint, and a weakness fell
on Cuchulain over Ferdiad there.

The story of the Tain is reflected in so many Gaelic names that at least a superficial knowledge of these events is necessary for a good understanding of the names. The Sons of Usnach and Deirdre ("The Sorrowful") were compatriots of Cuchulain and were among the first Irish settlers of Alban, to which land they fled to escape the King of Ulster. Later, in a deception, the King had the Sons slain in Ulster. Some time after that, Saint Columcille lost a great battle in the West and fled to Iona, from which point he and his missionaries made many conversions to Christianity in the Scottish mainland. By these assimilations, it is likely that all the breeds of dogs in Scotland and Ireland are related.

The lists of Gaelic names presented here were selected from ancient writings pertaining to the events discussed above and also from stories of the lives of saints, scholars, and poets.

J. A. K. D.

The Shetland Sheepdog, originally known on the Shetland Islands as the "Peerie" or "fairy" dog.   *Photo by Madelyn Cirinna.*

Contents

Can be construed to be Last Rites, by Sir Edwin Landseer, National Gallery, London.

1. Dogs of Celtic Origin

Nowhere in the world are animals loved more than they are in Ireland and Scotland. Objects of particular affection are dogs, horses, cattle, donkeys, and pigs. These species are to be seen throughout the country, but especially at the country fairs which occur almost every day of the year. The first society for the prevention of cruelty to animals arose in Ireland early in the nineteenth century, and today a great variety of organizations are actively devoted to the protection and improvement of animal life in Ireland.

From ancient times, the dogs, especially the Hounds of Ireland, were highly regarded throughout Europe and Asia, from which latter continent they probably came originally to the Emerald Isle. It is said that about the twelfth century B.C. a battle was fought at Moytura in which the Fomorians participated, accompanied by their Hounds, which bested all of the other dogs present.

The Irish Hounds, that is the Wolfhounds and the Greyhounds, were eagerly sought in Europe, and the Wolfhounds, especially, were looked upon as fabulous gifts when presented to friendly monarchs. From the earliest days, the Hound was accorded a great dignity in Ireland, which undoubtedly accounts for the dignified attitude of the Irish Wolfhound today.

Elsewhere in this work are separate sections on masculine names and feminine names. The rationale of the division of the names lies in the ancient history of Ireland, where queens vied for power with kings, and also lies in the customs of Ireland today, which maintains a largely matriarchal society, unique in modern times.

In such a society, founded upon the smallest unit of government—the family—it is natural that the close relationship would develop descriptive symbols such as the family coat-of-arms which has played an important role for centuries. Most of the old designs contain representations of a military nature, principally a sword in various postures. Some of the mottoes are drawn from a similar category, such as *Adjuvante Deo In Hostes*, translated "God's Help Before the Enemy." While most of the mottoes are in Latin, a substantial number are in

9

Gaelic, such as *Crom a Bu*, translated "Crom Forever." As may be expected, animals are frequently represented as further indication of the unmatched love of them by the Irish race.

It is somewhat surprising that the dog appears rarely as a symbol on crests and shields. Of those which bear likenesses of animals, by far the greatest number display a lion or lions—there being one hundred and eight which do. Second is the boar with twenty-two, followed by the salmon with fourteen, the snake with thirteen, the stag with twelve, and the eagle, the falcon, and the lizard with ten each. The wolf is represented by seven families—O'Callaghan, O'Crean, O'Flynn, Joyce, MacQuillen, Tully, and Woulfe. Among the dogs, only two breeds are included—the Greyhound, which is depicted on the coats-of-arms of the families of Broder, O'Fallon, O'Farrell, and MacGeoghegan, and the Irish Wolfhound, which appears only on the Crest of the McEnchroe, or Crowe, family.

Because of the predominance of the Greyhound and Terrier types in Ireland and Scotland and the great care taken over the centuries to preserve the purebred lines, there are not many breeds indigenous to these countries today. Descendants of the Greyhound type include the Irish Wolfhound and the Scottish Deerhound, which are closely related, first by Irish stock which traveled to Alban (Scotland) when the Irish settled there, and, secondly, by Scottish stock introduced by Captain George Augustus Graham, who was reviving the Irish Wolfhound when it was threatened with extinction in the nineteenth century.

"Don't turn your back on me." Scottish Terrier, from Jardine's *Naturalist's Library*: Dogs, Vol. II. 1840.

Scotch or rough Collie, "Blue," owned and photographed by Missy Green.

Cardigan Welsh Corgis. *Photo by Paulette Braun.*

2. A Listing of Celtic Dogs
(I) Irish   (S) Scottish

Aberdeen Terrier (S) (original name of Scottish Terrier)
Bearded Collie (S)
Border Collie (S)
Cairn Terrier (S)
Clydesdale Terrier (S) (former name of Skye Terrier)
Dandie Dinmont Terrier (S)
Glen of Imaal Terrier (I)
Gordon Setter (S)
Irish Greyhound (I)
Irish Setter (I)
Irish Terrier (I)
Irish Water Spaniel (I)
Irish Wolfhound (I)
Kerry Blue Terrier (I)
Norfolk Terrier (I) (S)
Norwich Terrier (I) (S) (same as Norfolk Terrier)
Paisley Terrier (S) (former name of Skye Terrier)
Rough Collie (S)
Scottish Collie (S)
Scottish Deerhound (S)
Scottish Greyhound (S) (same as Scottish Deerhound)
Scottish Terrier (S)
Shetland Sheepdog (S)
Skye Terrier (S)
Smooth Collie (S)
Soft-Coated Wheaten Terrier (I)
West Highland White Terrier (S)

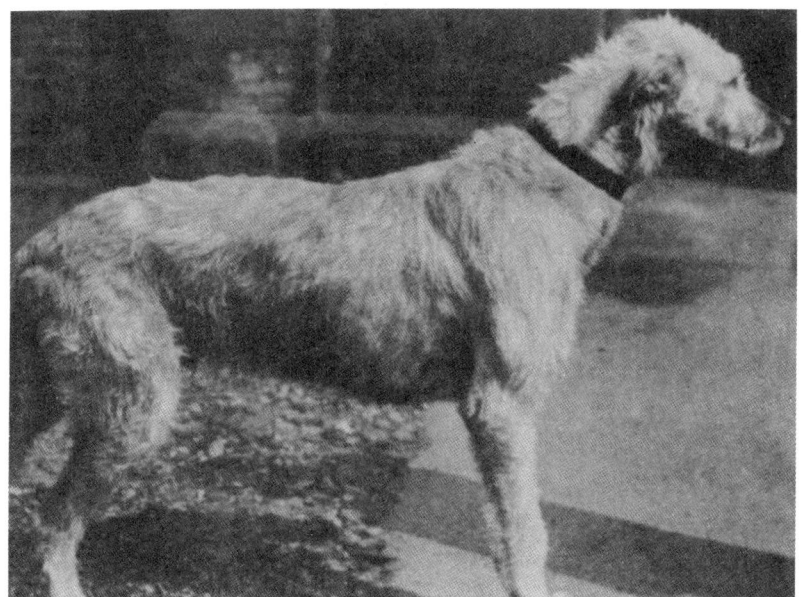

Ballyshannon, heroic Irish Wolfhound who was wounded in the trenches during World War I.

Kathleen, the first Irish Terrier shown in America. (New York, 1880.)

3. The Form of the Language

The Gaelic language is important to those who own dogs of Celtic origin—principally the dogs of Scotland and Ireland—because the identification of kennels and dogs in the show ring as being of such origin has the dual merit of associating them with their Celtic ancestry and of reminding the public of such association. This approach is the more important because, although the Gaelic language has very little resemblance to English, Gaelic surnames and first names often are the basis for names usually accepted as being of English origin. For instance, Johnson does not sound like an Irish surname, but it is, in fact, an Anglicization of McShain, or "Son of John"; nor does the surname Palmer have a discernible Irish tone, but it is somehow a translation into phonetic English of the Kerry County name of Mullover.

Gaelic, one of the basic languages of Europe, is elaborately expressive. The famous Irish actress Siobhan McKenna often maintained that the best English is spoken by the Irish. When asked to what reasons she ascribed this skill, she replied that for many generations the Irish were brought up on a much more intricate and expressive idiom—namely, the Gaelic. In the last three centuries, this skill also appears in the written word—for example, the works of George Bernard Shaw, William Butler Yeats, James Joyce, John Millington Synge, Oliver Goldsmith, Samuel Becket, Liam O'Flaherty, George Moore, Lord Dunsany, Oscar Wilde, Richard Brinsley Sheridan, Frank O'Connor, Sean O'Failain, Sean O'Casey, Lady Gregory, Edmund Burke, and Jonathan Swift, among others.

The noted sixteenth century geographer Nicholas Sanson, in his *Introduction a la Geographique des Langues,* wrote that the number of mother languages in Europe may be reduced to six—namely, Irish, Finlandish, Brettonic or Welsh, Biscayan, Hungarian, and Albanian. The Irish language, he wrote, was, besides in Ireland, still spoken in the North of Scotland. The Finlandish, according to Sanson, was spoken in Scandinavia, which he described as comprising Finland and Lapland. The Brettonic, the language of Lower Brittany in France, he

15

likewise called Welsh because it was the native language of Wales, which he called a province of England. The Biscayan, he said, was the language of Lower Navarre and Labour in France, and of Biscay in Spain. The Hungarian, in Sanson's words, was the language of Hungary and Transylvania, European countries which belonged to Turkey. And he noted that the Albanian language was named after Albania, also a European country which belonged to Turkey.

Another learned view is that of the sixteenth century scholar Joseph Scaliger, who held that there were eleven mother tongues in Europe— namely, Latin, Greek, Teutonic, Calvonic, Epirotic, Tartarian, Hungarian, Finlandish, Irish, Welsh, and Biscayan or Cantabrian.

The Milesians who were responsible for the origin of the Gaelic language did not employ the Roman letters. They used other marks or signs to represent speech sounds, including Oghumcrev and Oghumcoll. which were alphabetic characters composed of vertical lines, all named after trees and communicating sounds in accordance to their position on a horizontal line. This type of writing was said to be mysterious and used only by the druids in secret communication. It is not that secret today because the alphabetical form can be taught to anyone, Gaelic or otherwise, in the space of an hour.

It is maintained by some authorities that letters of the Roman alphabet were not introduced into Ireland and Scotland until they were brought there by Saint Patrick. This alphabet, likewise named after trees and vines, became known in Gaelic as Beith-Luis-Nion. It was charted in the following order:

Cairn Terrier. *Photo by Cindy Noland.*

Letter	Gaelic Name	English Equivalent
b	beithe	birch
l	luis	wild ash
f	fearn	alder
s	suil	willow
n	nion	ash
h	huath	white thorn
d	doire	oak
t	timne	unknown
c	coll	hazel
m	muin	vine
g	gort	ivy
p	peth-boc	unknown
r	ruis	elder
a	ailm	fir tree
o	onn	broom
u	ur	heath
e	edghadh	aspen
i	idho	yew

Border Collie working sheep.

While it is true that the Gaelic alphabet contains only seventeen letters (the h, an aspirate, being eliminated), the dual sounds of some of the consonants and the many diphthongs and triphthongs extend its literal form. The vowels are the same as the English a, e, i, o, and u; and the twelve consonants in the Gaelic alphabet are b, c, d, f, g, l, m, n, p, r, s, and t. Some of the letter forms, such as those representing the t and the g, are unlike the English alphabet and would be difficult for the unfamiliar reader to appreciate. To make this compilation more useful for the average reader, we are using the English forms of the letters.

As is true in the English language, a vowel in Gaelic can have either a short or a long sound. The long sounds of the vowels a, e, i, and o in Gaelic differ from the long sounds of these vowels in English, although the short sounds are the same. Examples of the short and long sounds of vowels in Gaelic are:

Vowel	Short	Long
a	pat	awl
e	pet	there
i	pit	seem
o	pot	ore
u	but	united

The principal diphthongs in Gaelic are ae, ao, eo, ia, and ua. While each is pronounced without a break, each also has a double sound which can be expressed as follows:

ae	bay
ao	aorta
eo	yeoman
ia	piano
ua	truant

The principal triphthongs in Gaelic are also five in number and are formed simply by adding the vowel i after each diphthong. Thus, the principal triphthongs are as follows:

aei
aoi
eoi
iai
uai

A fundamental rule in Gaelic is that governing "broad and slender" vowels. Under this rule broad and slender vowels may not be mixed—that is broad vowels must be with broad vowels and slender vowels with slender vowels. A, o, and u are broad vowels and e and i are slender vowels. The rule decrees that if a broad vowels precedes a consonant, then a vowel which follows that consonant must also be broad. Likewise, if a slender vowel precedes a consonant, then a vowel which follows that consonant must be slender.

As the terms imply, the slender is a short pronunciation, as in pat, while the broad is a long pronunciation, as in pate or pawt. Pronunciation in the Gaelic language is also aided by the use of accents placed over the syllables. The accents are various in form, but the dot is the one that is used most frequently. Accents are not used in this work because of difficulties involved in placing them above the English letters. To compensate for this lack, we have attempted to supply phonetic equivalents of Gaelic into English but are reminded that there is no English phonetic equivalent for some Gaelic words. The language is so far different from English that any phonetic approach is extremely difficult. Father Collier, O.M.I., in his scholarly and important book, *Irish Without Worry for Everyone*, has the modest comment, "Whether there is a corruption in the true sound of the Gaelic vowel, I must leave to experts on phonetics to decide."

The broad and slender rule extends also into the consonants so that the pronunciation of the consonant is affected by the nature of the vowel which follows. The most frequently used broad consonants are:

b   followed by a, pronounced bwa
c   the equivalent of k in English
d   a soft dh sound
f   pronounced fw
g   pronounced with the hard guh sound

l   not like l in English but with the tongue pushed between the front teeth
p   pronounced pw
r   pronounced with a vibrant rrr
s   pronounced like s in English
t   not like t in English but like th with the tongue against the upper teeth

The most frequently used slender consonants are:

b   as in bee
c   pronounced ky
d   pronounced much like the English d
f   pronounced much like the English f
g   pronounced as in give or get—always hard
l   pronounced like the English ll
n   pronounced like the English n with the tongue against the front teeth
p   pronounced like the English p
r   pronounced less burred than the broad r

Now that you have been indoctrinated in the rule of "broad with broad and slender with slender," all you need do is recognize broad and slender when they occur. It is not easy. Even more than with other languages, you must hear the Irish language and speak it before you can become at all proficient in its usage. It is often said, and with some authority, that you cannot fully learn an additional language after you have passed thirty-five years of age. Gaelic is very difficult to learn. Inquiry addressed to a scholar who is skilled in Russian and who had delved into Gaelic, as to which of these two is more difficult, elicited the response that the Gaelic is much more difficult.

Then there are, as in every language, exceptions to the rules. There are also the aspirates and the labial, palatal, and dental sounds.

B at the beginning of a word, followed by a broad vowel, is pronounced w; if followed by a slender vowel, it has the sound of v.
F aspirated becomes silent.

An initial aspirate m followed by a broad vowel has the sound of w; in the middle of a word and followed by a slender vowel, m has the sound of v.

Whether broad or slender, p aspirated has the sound of f.

T aspirated and followed by a broad vowel has the sound of th, and followed by a slender vowel, is pronounced like y.

Eclipsing and eclipsed consonants pose another threat to successful pronunciation, since they occur with regularity. The eclipsable consonants are b, c, d, f, g, p, and t, and those capable of eclipsing are j, g, n, b, and d. Consonants are eclipsed when they are in pairs, the eclipsing consonant appearing before the eclipsed consonant and changing the sound to that of the eclipsing consonant. A few examples are gc, bp, mb, nd, and so on.

All Gaelic was the same when it was introduced into Ireland and then into Scotland when Irish invaders made their way into the nearby province of Ulster in the fifth century, and to the Isle of Man (probably from Scotland) at a later date. The language remained uniformly the same through the ninth century, after which changes, at first slight and then progressive, were noted in the Scottish and Manx versions. As a result of religious influences from England, Manx has been, from the seventeenth century, based upon a combination of Gaelic and English and favors the sound of the latter.

Scottish Gaelic in the spoken word began to diverge from the Irish Gaelic about the tenth century, but the written language remained the same until sometime in the seventeenth century. As of today, the principal feature which the two forms have in common is a large vocabulary, especially the written vocabulary. The Scottish version now has varied to a degree from the Irish version in construction and sound, partaking of old English and Scandinavian forms, while the Irish forms have remained the same except for certain infusions of words of French and English origin. For this reason, the Gaelic spoken in Ireland is now largely referred to merely as Irish. There was a great movement to revive the Irish language in Ireland to compete with English after the 1916 Easter Rising and the subsequent invasion by English mercenaries known as The Black and Tans.

For some years under various governments of the Republic of Ireland, the study of Gaelic was made compulsory in all schools and universities. In a similar effort, any applicant for a position in the government or in any school or university, was required to have fairly good proficiency in the Gaelic language. This requirement was abandoned after the defeat of Premier Jack Lynch, a Corkman, in the 1973 elections in the Republic. He has since been reelected but the language requirement has not been reinstituted.

For several generations the real concentration of people using the Gaelic or Irish language has been in an area known as the Gaeltacht. During the years that the study of Gaelic was compulsory, Gaeltacht's support of the Gaelic idiom was provided through many elements, including the fact that one of the ministers, or cabinet members in these regimes, had a dual capacity—that of Minister for Lands and that of representing the Gaeltacht or Gaelic-speaking part of the country. (It is interesting to note that there is also a Gaeltacht in Argentina in South America.)

Irish humorist-commentator Brian O'Nolan, who wrote under the pen names Flann O'Brien and Myles na Gopaleen, provided the following description of the Irish language:

"A lady lecturing on the Irish language drew attention to the fact (I mentioned it myself as long ago as 1925) that, while the average English speaker gets along with a mere 400 words, the Irish-speaking peasant uses 4000. Considering what most English speakers can achieve with their tiny fund of noises, it is a nice speculation to what extremity one would be reduced if one were locked up for a day with an Irish-speaking bore. . . .

"My point, however, is this. The 400/4000 ratio is fallacious; 400/400,000 would be more like it. There is scarcely a single word in the Irish (barring, possibly, SASSANACH*) that is simple and explicit. Apart from words with endless shades of cognate meaning, there are many with so complete a spectrum of graduated ambiguity that each of them can be made to express two directly contrary meanings, as well as a plethora of intermediate concepts that have no bearing on either. And all this strictly within the linguistic field. Superimpose on all that the miasma of ironic usage, poetic license, oxymoron, plamas, Celtic evasion, Irish bullery and Paddy Whackery, and it is a sage bet that you will find yourself very far from home."

Since this book is intended for use in naming dogs and kennels, all words included in the listings and all Gaelic equivalents have been capitalized, even though they might not ordinarily be capitalized when used in some other context.

For convenience and fluency, the listings are arranged in the order of the English alphabet, and the characters of the English (rather than the Gaelic) alphabet are used in the Gaelic equivalents.

*"Sassanach" is an Irish insulting name for an Englishman.

22

Irish Wolfhound, Ch. Donchadd of Baileglas, at Morgantown, West
Virginia, July 1978. Owners, Dr. and Mrs. Lawrence Kenny.
Gordon Setter, Ch. Afternod Yank of Rockaplenty, at the Mid-West
Specialty in Trumbull, Ohio. Breeder—Owner, Mrs. William Clark.

Soft Coated Wheaten Terrier. *Photo by Bill Butler.*

4. General Alphabetic Listing
(English-Gaelic)

English	Gaelic	Phonetic

A

English	Gaelic	Phonetic
Able	Cumasac	Koomasak
Above	Luas	Loos
Absolute	Ceart	Kart
Ace	An T-aon	Awn Thayon
Acres	Acra	Awkra
Adorable	Adrad	Awdrawd
Adventurer	Fear Fiuntair	Feer Fweentair
Affable	Lac	Lok
Affectionate	Geana	Gonna
Agile	Lut	Lthoot
Agriculture	Ar	Awr
Ale	Lionn	Lthon
All	Go Leir	Guh Leer
Along	Ar Fead	Awr Fwad
And	Agus	Awgus
Angel	Aingeal	Angawl
Animal	Ainmi	Awnmee
Arrogant	Diomsac	Dthomsak
Artist	Ealaionta	Eelontha
Attraction	Taraing	Thawrong
Award	An Craob	Awn Kraw

English	Gaelic	Phonetic

B

English	Gaelic	Phonetic
Baby (mas.)	Leanb	Lheen
Baby (fem.)	Bunoc	Boonowk
Back	Drom	Dhrom
Badge	Comarta	Komawtha
Badger	Broc	Brok
Bagpipes	Piob	Peoob
Ball	Liatroid	Leeatrwa
Ballad	Amran	Awmran
Band	Banda	Bwawnda
Bar	Barra	Bwawrra
Bard	Bard	Bwarrd
Barker	Sceanail	Skeenl
Bark of Dog	Sceam	Skam
Barley	Corna	Korna
Baron	Barun	Bawroon
Barrel	Barraille	Bawrrall
Beacon	Leas Comarta	Lees Komawrtha
Beam (of wood)	Sail	Sail
Bear	Beitir	Beetirr
Bear	Beoir	Bore
Beast	Ainmi	Aynmi
Beautiful	Alainn	Alaween
Bee	Beac	Bake
Beetle	Priompallan	Pwrompallan
Bell-Ringer	Fear Cloig	Feer Klog
Beloved	Dilis	Dheelis
Below	Tios	Teeos
Berry	Caor	Kore
Best	Is Fearr	Iss Feerr
Bet	Geall	Guhall
Big	Mor	More
Biscuit	Briosca	Broska
Bishop	Easpag	Eespaguh
Bittersweet	Searb-Milis	Seerv-Meelis

26

English	Gaelic	Phonetic
Blarney	Blarney	Blarnee
Boat	Bad	Bwawd
Boisterous	Garb	Gawrbh
Body	Colann	Kowlawn
Bog	Portac	Pwortak
Bold	Dana	Dhawnaw
Bomb	Bomba	Bomba
Bone	Cnam	Konawm
Bonnet	Bairread	Bwarreed
Book	Leadar	Lleedar
Bottle	Burdeal	Burdeel
Bouncing	Preab	Pwreeb
Bountiful	Fluirseac	Fwloorsak
Bow	Boga	Bowgaw
Box	Bosca	Boskaw
Bran	Bran	Bran
Brass	Pras	Pwras
Brave	Calma	Kallmaw
Brazen	Neam-Naireac	Ntheem-Nawrrak
Bread	Aran	Aran
Breakfast	Bricfeasta	Brekfast
Breeze	Loitne	Lloothna
Brewer	Bribeir	Brreebar
Bride	Brideac	Brydak
Bright	Geal	Guhail
Bronze	Cre-Uma	Kreeooma
Brook	Srutan	Srootawn
Broth	Anrait	Awnrray
Bucket	Buicead	Buukad
Burn	Do	Do
Butler	Im	Im
Butterfly	Peidleacan	Pweedelkawn
Buttermilk	Blatac	Bthawtak
Buttons	Cnaipe	Knape

English	Gaelic	Phonetic
	C	
Cabbage	Cabaiste	Kawbawthe
Cake	Bairin	Bayreen
Camel	Camal	Kamel
Canal	Canail	Kanawl
Candidate	Iarrtoir	Eearrtoorr
Candle	Comneal	Komneel
Cannon	Gunna Mor	Guhnna More
Cap	Caipin	Kaypwin
Captain	Captaen	Kapthin
Captive	Cime	Kym
Caraway	Carabue	Karaboo
Card	Carta	Karta
Caress	Barrog	Bwarrog
Carrot	Meacan Dearg	Maykan Derguh
Cart	Cairt	Kart
Castle	Caislean	Kasleen
Caterpillar	Cnum	Konoom
Cauliflower	Colais	Kolays
Celebration	Gasra	Guhasrra
Celebrity	Duine Morclu	Dhueen Morekloo
Celery	Meacan Tataba	Maykan Thawthaba
Cent	Cead	Kad
Chafer	Daol	Dhol
Charm	Brioct	Brroct
Checkmate	Faireann Ficeall	Fwareen Fwikall
Cheer	Gair	Guhair
Cheerful	Suairc	Sooark
Cheese	Cais	Kawse
Cherry	Silin	Sileen
Chew	Cogaint	Koganth
Chief	Ceannasai	Kannarrsi
Child	Leanb	Lheen
Chips	Sliseog	Slleeslog
Chocolate	Seaclaid	Sayklaw

English	Gaelic	Phonetic
Choir	Cor	Kore
Chop	Easna	Essna
Chorus	Curfa	Koorfaw
Christmas	Nollaig	Nollaguh
Church	Eaglais	Ayglis
Cider	Lionn Ull	Lon Wool
Circus	Siorcus	Sirkus
City	Baile	Bwalla
Clam	Briollacan	Brrollakawn
Clan	Clann	Klan
Class	Rant	Rant
Classic	Clasagac	Kllasagak
Clergyman	Cleireac	Kleerak
Cliff	Faill	Fwall
Clip	Bearrad	Beerad
Cloud	Scamall	Skamall
Clown	Amadan	Amadawn
Club	Cleit	Kleet
Clue	Lide	Lleed
Clumsy	Tutac	Thootak
Coach	Coiste	Kooste
Coat	Cota	Kowta
Cock	Coileac	Kowlak
Cockle	Ruacan	Rrookan
Cockroach	Daol	Dhawl
Codfish	Trosc	Throsk
Coffee	Caife	Kaffay
Coin	Bonn	Bown
Cold	Fuact	Fwook
Colleen	Cailin	Kailleen
College	Colaiste	Kolawstha
Colonel	Cornal	Kernal
Comet	Realt Eireabaill	Rrawlt Eerbowl
Comical	Greannmar	Guhrranmar
Command	Ordu	Orrdoo
Commandant	Ceannfeadna	Kannfadhna
Committeeman	Coisteoir	Koystha

English	Gaelic	Phonetic
Company	Cuideacta	Koodaktha
Concert	Cuirm Ceoil	Koorm Kail
Congress	Comdail	Komdall
Consent	Toiliu	Tholoo
Consort	Ceile	Kaylee
Conspiracy	Comceilg	Komkolg
Constable	Constabla	Konstabel
Contented	Sasam	Sawsam
Cook	Cocaire	Kowkair
Copper	Copar	Koparr
Cordial (liqueur)	Deoc Meisce	Dhok Mesh
Cork	Corc	Kork
Corn	Arbar	Arrbarr
Cottage	Teac	Taik
Country	Tir	Teer
County	Contae	Kowntee
Courage	Misneac	Misnak
Courageous	Misniuil	Mishnool
Course	Cursa	Kurrsa
Court	Cuirt	Kurt
Crayfish	Peardog	Pairdowguh
Creek	Srut	Srooth
Cress	Biolar	Bilarr
Crest	Cirin	Kirin
Cricket	Creagar	Kreegarr
Crier	Callaire	Kallarr
Crock	Proca	Prowka
Crocodile	Crogal	Krogal
Crooked	Lubta	Looptha
Crystal	Criostal	Kristal
Cup	Cupan	Koopawn
Currants	Corainti	Koorrantee
Cut	Gearrad	Guheerrad

English	Gaelic	Phonetic
	D	
Daddy-Long-Legs	Pilib A Geitire	Pwilib Aw Geether
Dainty	Gleoite	Guhleeth
Dale	Gleann	Guhleen
Dam (mother)	Matair	Mawther
Dance	Rince	Rrinse
Dancer	Rinceoir	Rrinser
Dandy	Gaige	Guhaig
Dark	Dorcadas	Dhorkas
Darling	Muirnin	Mourneen
Dear	A Gra	Aw Graw
Deep	Doimin	Dhowmeen
Deer	Fia	Fwya
Delegate	Teacta	Thekta
Delight	Atas	Awthas
Delightful	Aoibinn	Owbeen
Demonstrate	Leiriu	Leeroo
Desirable	Inmianaite	Eenanithee
Destiny	Cinniuint	Kinoonth
Detective	Bleactaire	Blakthair
Devil	Diabal	Dhiable
Dictator	Deactoir	Dhekthor
Dignified	Dignitiuil	Dhignithool
Din	Fotrom	Fwotrom
Diplomat	Taroleoir	Tarolor
Director	Stuirtoir	Stoorthor
Divine	Diata	Dhitha
Doe	Eilit	Eilith
Dog	Madra	Madra
Dormouse	Dallaman	Dhallameen
Double	Dubalta	Dhoobaltha
Down	Sios	Seyos
Dozing	Ag Miorarnaig	Awg Myornag
Dream	Briongloro	Brronglowro
Dress	Eadac	Eedak

31

English	Gaelic	Phonetic
Drop	Deoc	Dhok
Druid	Drai	Dhrray
Drum	Dord	Dhord
Drummer	Drumadoir	Dhrumadore
Dusk	Feascar	Feskar
Dust	Smurd	Smoorrd
Dutiful	Umall	Oomall
Dynamite	Diona	Dhiona

E

Eager	Fonnmar	Fwonmar
Earl	Iarla	Eerrla
Ears	Cluas	Klooas
Earwig	Gaillseao	Guhallso
East	An T-oirtear	Awn Tortheer
Easy	Furasta	Fwoorastha
Echo	Macalla	Makalla
Eclipse	Uru	Oorroo
Elegant	Maisiuil	Maysul
Elf	Siofra	Showfrra
Eminence	Ard	Awrd
Empire	Impreact	Eemprakt
Enchantment	Draioct	Dhrayk
Enormous	Ri-Mor	Rye-More
Estate	Eastat	Eesthath
Evil	Docar	Dhokarr
Excellent	Tar Barr	Tharr Barr
Excited	Corraite	Korrathe
Expert	Eolac	Olak
Exquisite	Sireactac	Seerraktak
Extraordinary	Neam-Coitanta	Ntheem-Kowthantha
Extravagant	Ro-Caiteac	Row-Kaytak
Extreme	Forceann	Fworkan
Eyes	Suil	Sweel

English	Gaelic	Phonetic
	F	
Fabulous	Aisteac	Aysthok
Fair	Aonac	Ownthak
Fairy	Siofra	Seefwrra
Faithful	Dilis	Dheelis
Famous	Clumail	Klhoomal
Fancy	Samlu	Samloo
Fantastic	Aisteac	Aysthok
Farm	Feirm	Farm
Fashionplate	Mod	Mode
Fast	Troscad	Thrroskad
Fat	Bionag	Beenog
Fawn	Fia Og	Fwya Og
Feather	Caeite	Kathee
Felicitous	Sona	Sona
Female	Baineann	Bwaneen
Ferret	Firead	Fweeraid
Fickle	Guagac	Guguhk
Fiddle	Berolin	Beerowlin
Field	Pairc	Pwark
Fife	Froeog	Fwrrog
Fight	Troro	Thrrorro
Finished	Criocnaite	Kreenath
Fish	Iasc	Ishk
Flag	Bratac	Brathak
Flaming	Lasair	Lhasar
Flaring	Lascad	Lhaskad
Flask	Flaigin	Fwlhageen
Fleece	Lomra	Lhomrra
Fleet	Luat	Llooth
Fleet-footed	Mear	Mair
Flight	Teitead	Theethad
Flint	Cloc Tine	Klok Theen
Flounder	Leatog	Lheetog
Flourishing	Fe Blat	Fwe Blhath
Flute	Feadog	Fweedog

English	Gaelic	Phonetic
Fly	Cuil	Kool
Fog	Ceo	Ko
Followers	Luct	Lhuk
Fond	Cion	Kion
Foolish	Amadantuil	Amadhthool
Fore	Roim	Rrom
Foreign	Iasacta	Eesaktha
Foremost	Tosaig	Thosag
Forest	Foraois	Fworros
Fortress	Dun	Dhoon
Fortunate	Amarac	Awmarrak
Fountain	Tobar	Thobwarr
Fox	Sionnac	Shonthak
Foxy	Glic	Guhlhik
Free	Saor	Sar
Freedom	Saorise	Sarees
Friar	Bratair	Brrawtor
Frog	Loscann	Lhoskan
Front	Tosac	Thosak
Fruit	Torad	Thorrad
Full	Lan	Lhawn
Fun	Greann	Guhrran
Funny	Greannmar	Guhrranmar
Fur	Fionnad	Fweenad
Fury	Ar Buile	Awrr Bweel

G

English	Gaelic	Phonetic
Gait	Imeact	Eemak
Gallant	Misniuil	Meeshweel
Galloping	Ar Cosa-in-Airde	Awrr Kos-in-Air
Gambler	Cearrbac	Karrbak
Game	Cluice	Kithoos
Gate	Geata	Guhata
Gay	Suarc	Swarrk

34

English	Gaelic	Phonetic
Gentlemen	Fir	Fweer
Ghost	Taibse	Thaybs
Giant	Fatac	Fwathak
Gingerbread	Sinsear Aran	Seensarr Arrawn
Gipsy	Giofog	Guhofwowguh
Girl	Gearrcaile	Guharrkall
Glade	Gleann	Guhleen
Glamor	Meall	Meel
Glamorous	Mealltac	Meelthak
Glare	Lonrad	Lhonrrad
Gleaming	Lonrad	Lhonrrad
Glen	Gleann	Guhleen
Glorious	Glormar	Guhlhormarr
Glowing	Lonrac	Lhonrak
Gnat	Mioltog	Meethoguh
Gnome	Gnome	Guhnome
Goblin	Puca	Pwooka
God	Dia	Dheea
Goddess	Baindia	Bwandheea
Going	Meact	Meeakth
Gold	Or	Owrr
Good	Mait	Math
Gooseberry	Spionan	Spweenawn
Gorgeous	Sar-Alain	Sawrr Althan
Government	Rialtas	Rreelthas
Graceful	Grastuit	Guhrrasthwooth
Graduate	Ceimi	Kaymy
Grand	Brea	Brra
Grape	Caor	Kor
Grateful	Buioc	Booik
Gravel	Grean	Guhrran
Great	Mor	More
Grog	Uisce Beata	Wiska Batha
Ground (soil)	Talam	Thalam
Growling	Drannad	Dhrrannad
Guide	Treorai	Thrrorray
Gun	Guna	Guhoona

English	Gaelic	Phonetic
	H	
Haddock	Cadog	Kadowguh
Hairy	Gruagac	Guhrrooguhak
Half	Leat	Lhat
Halfpenny	Leitpingin	Lheethpwinguhin
Halibut	Alabard	Alhabwarrd
Ham	Mas	Mays
Hand (cards)	Carta	Kartha
Handsome	Doiciuil	Dhokool
Happy	Sona	Sona
Hard	Cruaid	Krood
Harmony	Comcordad	Komkorrdhad
Harp	Clairseac	Klhairrsak
Haughty	Morcuis	Morrkoos
Haunted	Ionad Gnait	Onad Guhnait
Head Man	Fear Cinn	Feer Kin
Heart	Croi	Krroy
Heartily	Croiuil	Krroyl
Heath	Fraoc Min	Fwrrak Meen
Heather	Fraoc Min	Fwrrak Meen
Heavenly	Neime	Ntheem
Hedgehog	Grainneog	Guhrrannoguh
Henchman	Comguailli	Komguhoolhi
Hero	Gaiscioc	Guhaiskok
Herring	Scadan	Skadawn
High	Ard	Awrd
Highland	Ard Talam	Awrd Thalam
Highland Fling	Ard Talam Rince	Awrd Thalam Rrinse
High Road	Botar	Bowtharr
Highway	Botar	Bowtharr
Highwayman	Bitiunic	Beetoonik
Hill	Cnoc	Konok
Hilt	Dorncar	Dhorrnkarr
Hole	Poll	Pwole
Hollow	Lagan	Lthagawn

36

English	Gaelic	Phonetic
Home	Baile	Bwalla
Honey	Mil	Meel
Honor	Onoir	Owneer
Honorable	Ongrac	Ownguhrrak
Hope	Docas	Dhowkas
Hopeful	Docasac	Dhowkasak
Hornpipe	Cornpioppa	Kornpweepa
Horse	Capall	Kapall
Hot	Te	The
Hound	Cu	Koo
House	Teac	Tak
Howl	Glam	Guhlham
Humble	Umal	Oomalh
Humorous	Greannmar	Guhrranmar
Hunting	Fiac	Feeak
Hussy	Stiusai	Sthusy

I

Ideal	Barr-Samail	Bwarr-Samall
Identical	Ionann	Ownan
Idol	Fol	Fol
Illustrious	Oireac	Orak
Image	Iomaig	Eemaguh
Imitation	Aitris	Aythris
Immaculate	Gan Smal	Guhn Smawl
Immediate	Laitreac	Lawthrak
Imminent	Ag Teact	Awg Thakth
Imp	Mac Mioscaise	Mak Meeskase

37

English	Gaelic	Phonetic
Important	Tabactac	Tawbwakthak
Impresario	Stiurtoir	Sthoorthoor
Independent	Neam-Spleac	Name-Spwlawk
Individual	Duine	Dhween
Infant (mas.)	Naionan	Nayonawn
Infant (fem.)	Bunoc	Boonowk
Innocent	Neam Ciontac	Name Kionthak
Intelligence	Intleact	Eenthlhakth
Intrepid	Calma	Kallmaw
Iron	Iarann	Irron
Irresistible	Do-Diongbala	Dho-Dhongbwala
Island	Oilean	Oolawn

J

English	Gaelic	Phonetic
Jesting	Magad	Maguhad
Job	Obair	Owbwair
Jockey	Marcac	Markak
Joke	Abact	Abakth
Jolly	Suairc	Sooarrk
Joy	Atas	Awthas
Joyful	Atasac	Awthasak
Jubilant	Atasac	Awthasak
Judge (noun)	Breiteam	Breetheem
Jug	Crusca	Krrooska
Jump	Leim	Leem
Jumper	Leimi	Leemee
Junior	Soisear	Sowsare
Justice	Coir	Koor

English	*Gaelic*	*Phonetic*
	K	
Keen	Gear	Guheer
Keeper	Coimeadai	Koymawdaw
Keepsake	Seoid Cuimne	Sead Koomne
Kennel	Cro	Krow
Kettle	Ciotal	Kettel
Key	Eocair	Eekarr
Kindly	Sagas	Sagas
King	Rhi	Rrhi
Kingdom	Rioct	Rreeokth
Kiss	Pog	Powg
Kitten	Caitin	Kaytin
Knight	Ridire	Rridhirre
Knoll	Cnoc	Konok
	L	
Lace	Lasa	Llawsa
Lad	Garsun	Guharrsoon
Lady	Bear Uasal	Beer Wishal
Lake	Loc	Lok
Lamb	Uan	Ween
Lamp	Lampa	Lampa
Lance	Lann	Lann
Lane	Boitrin	Boythrrin
Lass	Cailin	Kaylin
Last	Deirid	Dherid

English	Gaelic	Phonetic
Laughing	Ag Gairi	Awg Gayrree
Lawyer	Fear Dli	Feer Dhlee
Lea	Ban	Bwawn
Leader	Treorai	Trrorray
Leg	Cos	Kos
Legend	Sean-Sceal	Shawn-Skeel
Lemon	Liomord	Leemoorrd
Leprechaun	Liopracan	Leeprakawn
Lesson	Ceact	Kakt
Lettuce	Leitis	Lettus
Light (in color)	Eadrom	Eedhrrom
Lion	Leon	Lleon
Liquor	Lact	Lakth
Listen	Eistreact	Eisthrrakth
Listener	Eistiteor	Eisthithorr
Litter	Al	Awl
Little	Beag	Beg
Lobster	Gliomac	Guhlomak
Lofty	Ard	Awrd
Lone	Aonair	Onair
Lonely	Uaigneas	Weeguhnas
Long	Fada	Fawda
Look	Feacaint	Feekant
Looking	Feac Ar	Feek Awr
Lord	Tiarna	Theerna
Lovable	Geanuit	Guhanweeth
Love	Gra	Guhrraw
Lover	Leannan	Leenawn
Loving	Grac	Guhrrawk
Lowland	Geim Talam	Guheem Thalam
Low Road	Geim Botar	Guheem Bothawrr
Luck	Ad	Awd
Lucky	Aduil	Adweel
Luxuriant	Souil	Soweel
Lying (reclining)	Ar Sleaslui	Awr Sleesloo
Lyric	Liric	Leerrik

English	Gaelic	Phonetic
	M	
Mackerel	Ronnac	Rronnak
Magic	Draioct	Dhrrawokth
Magistrate	Guistis	Guhoosthis
Magnetic	Admaintac	Adhmanthak
Magnificent	Sar-Alainn	Sawrr-Awlann
Maiden	Maigdean	Maguhdan
Majestic	Morga	Moorguha
Male	Fireannac	Fweernak
Man	Fir	Fweer
Mark	Comarta	Komarrtha
Marshal	Marascal	Marraskal
Marvellous	Iontac	Younthak
Master	Maistir	Mawsther
Masterpiece	Sar Ealai	Sawrr Eelaw
Mate (noun)	Pairti	Pwarrthee
Mayor	Maor	Maorr
Meadow	Momear	Mowmeer
Medal	Bonn	Bonn
Member	Ball	Bwall
Memorable	Buan Cluil	Boon Klweel
Memory	Cuimne	Koomne
Merriment	Meidir	Madhir
Merry	Meidreac	Madhrrak
Metal	Miotal	Meethal
Metallic	Miotail	Meethal
Mile	Mile	Meel
Military	Arm	Arrm
Million	Milliun	Milloon
Millionaire	Milliunai	Milloonai
Mine	Mianac	Meenak
Miner	Mianadoir	Meenadhoor
Mineral	Mianrai	Meenrrai
Minor	Mionur	Meenoorr
Minstrel	Piobaire	Pweebwarr

English	Gaelic	Phonetic
Mischievous	Mioscais	Meeskas
Mist	Ceo	Ko
Mistress	Maistreas	Mawsthrraws
Modest	Moduil	Modhweel
Monarch	Rhi	Rrhi
Moon	Gealac	Guhlak
Moonbeam	Bioma Gealac	Bwoma Guhlak
Moor	Mointean	Mownthain
More	Breis	Brress
Most	Is	Iss
Mountain	Cnoc	Konok
Mouse	Luc	Look
Mouth	Beal	Beel
Movement	Corrail	Korrail
Much	Moran	Moorawn
Muffin	Toirtin	Torrtean
Mule	Miuil	Mule
Mushroom	Fas-Aon-Oice	Fwaws-An-Owke
Musician	Ceoltoir	Keltoorr
Mussel	Iascan	Yaskawn
My	Mo	Muh
Mystery	Rundiamair	Rroondhiamair
Mystic	Diamair	Dhiamair

N

English	Gaelic	Phonetic
Naked	Noct	Nokth
Name	Ainm	Ainm
Namesake	Fear Darb Ainm	Feer Dharb Ainm
Native	Ducais	Dhookas
Natural	Nadurta	Nawhurtha
Naughty	Dana	Dhawna
Nautical	Loingseoract	Lhonguhsorrakth

English	Gaelic	Phonetic
Navigator	Loingseoracta	Lhonguhsorraktha
Neat	Deas	Dhees
New	Nua	Nua
Newsboy	Paipear Garsun	Pwayperr Guharrsoon
Nice	Deas	Dhees
Nimble	Lufar	Lhoofwar
No	Ni	Nee
Noble	Uasal	Wasal
Noisy	Glorac	Guhloorrak
Normal	Gnatac	Guhnawthak
North	Tuaid	Thooaid
Nose	Sron	Sroon
Novel (adjective)	Nua	Nua
Nut	Cno	Konoo

O

Obedient	Umal	Oomal
Object (purpose)	Abar	Abwarr
Obstinate	Ceanntrean	Kawnthrreen
Officer	Oifigeac	Ofwiguhek
Old	Aosta	Aostha
Operator	Obriteoir	Obrithorr
Opera	Ceoldrama	Koldhrrawma
Orchestra	Ceolfuireann	Kalthfwooreen
Ore	Mianac	Meenak
Organ (music)	Organ	Orguhawn
Otter	Dobarcu	Dhobwarrku
Our	Ar	Awr
Outcast	Dibeartac	Dheybeerthak
Outlaw	Meirleac	Marelhak
Oyster	Oisre	Oiser

43

English	Gaelic	Phonetic
	P	
Paddock	Tuar	Thuar
Pagan	Paganac	Pwawguhawnak
Painter	Deannaire	Deenair
Pan	Beiste	Beesty
Pants (noun)	Trius	Thrroos
Parade	Mor Suil	More Sweel
Paradise	Paratas	Pwarrathas
Paramount	Priom	Pwrreyom
Parishioner	Paroisteanac	Pwarrowstheenak
Parliament	Dail	Dhall
Partner	Pairti	Pwarrthi
Passenger	Paisinear	Pwassineer
Patches	Paiste	Pwasty
Patience	Foigne	Fwoyguhne
Patient	Otar	Othar
Pawn	Ar Geall	Awr Guheel
Peaceful	Siocanta	Showkantha
Peach	Peitseog	Pweethsog
Pear	Piorra	Pweeorra
Pebble	Purog	Pwoorruguh
Peddler	Mangaire	Manguhair
Pennant	Bratac	Brrathak
Pepper	Piobar	Pweeobwar
Perfect	Lan-Ceart	Lhawn-Karth
Pet	Peata	Pweetha
Philosopher	Feallsam	Fweelhsam
Pickle	Picil	Pikil
Pick-up	Piocad	Pwokad
Picture	Pictiuir	Pwikthure
Pie	Piog	Pweeogh
Pike	Pice	Pwike
Pilot	Piolot	Pweelhowth
Pineapple	Anann	Anann
Pint	Piunt	Pwiunth

44

English	Gaelic	Phonetic
Pipes	Piob	Pweeob
Pirate	Foglai Mara	Fwoglhee Mara
Place (noun)	Ait	Aweeth
Plaice (fish)	Leatog	Lheethog
Planet	Plamead	Pwlameed
Playboy	Buacaill Baire	Boukhal Bwawrr
Playful	Cleaseac	Klheesak
Pleasant	Suairc	Swark
Pleasure	Aoibneas	Awbness
Plentiful	Fluirseac	Fwthweelrsak
Plough	Ceacta	Keektha
Plum	Pluma	Pwlhooma
Poem	Dan	Dhawn
Poet	File	Fwilhe
Poetry	Filioct	Fwilheokth
Poker	Bior Tine	Biorr Thin
Pole	Cuaille	Kooale
Policeman	Garda	Guharda
Political	Polaitioct	Pwolatheeokth
Pompous	Poimpiuil	Pwompweelh
Pond	Locan	Lhokawn
Porcupine	Graineog	Guhrawnoguh
Porpoise	Muc Mara	Muk Mara
Post	Staic	Sthake
Potato	Prata	Pwraytee
Powder	Pudar	Pwoodhar
Power	Cumact	Kumakth
Powerful	Cumactac	Kumakthak
Practical	Praiticiuil	Pwrathikooth
Praise	Molad	Molhad
Praiseworthy	Inmolta	Inmolhtha
Precious	Luacmar	Lhooakmarr
President	Uactaran	Uactharan
Pretty	Deas	Dhees
Prince	Flait	Fwllath
Princess	Banflait	Bwanfwllath

English	Gaelic	Phonetic

English	Gaelic	Phonetic
Prize	Duais	Dhuas
Profession	Gairm Beata	Guharm Beetha
Professor	Ollam	Ollam
Promise	Gealluint	Guhalloonth
Pudding	Putog	Pwutowguh
Pupil	Macleirn	Makleern
Puppy	Coilean	Kolleen

Q

English	Gaelic	Phonetic
Quadruped	Ceatarcosac	Katharkosak
Quaint	Ait	Ait
Queen	Bainrion	Bawnreen
Quick	Tapaid	Thapwadh
Quicksilver	Airgead Beo	Arguhad Beo
Quiet	Cneasta	Konastha

R

English	Gaelic	Phonetic
Racing	Ras	Raws
Radiant	Soilseac	Soilhsak
Raider	Foglai	Fwoglhai
Rain	Baisteac	Bwasthak
Rainbow	Boga Sine	Boguh Seen
Raisin	Risin	Risin
Random	Fain	Fwawn
Rapid	Tapaid	Thapwadh
Rare	Tearc	Therk
Ready	Ullam	Ullam
Rebel	Meirleac	Marelak
Refuge	Dion	Dhion
Regal	Rioga	Rreeoguha
Rejoicing	Lucair	Lhookawr

English	Gaelic	Phonetic
Reluctance	Neam-Fonn	Neam Fwonn
Remarkable	Sundasac	Sundhasak
Representative	Ionadai	Yonadhee
Reptile	Piast	Pwiasth
Republic	Publact	Pwublhakth
Retrieve	Fail	Fwail
Return	Fillead	Fwilladh
Revolutionary	Granna	Guhrawna
Reward	Duais	Dhuas
Rhubarb	Biabog	Biabowguh
Ribbon	Ribin	Ribeen
Rice	Ris	Rees
Rich	Saibir	Saibir
Rider	Marcac	Markak
Ridge	Iomaire	Yomair
Rifle	Rifil	Reefl
Right	Ceart	Karth
Ringleader	Cinnire	Kinnire
Ripple	Cuilitini	Kweelhitheenee
Rising	Tus	Thoos
Rival	Iomateoir	Yomathor
River	Aba	Aba
Road	Botar	Bowtharr
Robber	Bitiunac	Bithoonak
Rock	Carraig	Karraguh
Rocky	Carraigeac	Karraguhak
Rogue	Rogaire	Rroguhair
Roll	Rotlu	Rothloo
Rook (chess)	Preacan	Pwrreekawn
Rosary	An Corom Muire	An Korom Mweer
Royal	Rioga	Rreeoguha
Ruffian	Coiripeac	Korripwak
Ruler	Railaiteoir	Rrailaithor
Running	Reatac	Rreethak
Rustic	Fear Tuaite	Feer Thuathe
Rye	Seagal	Seeguhalh

English	Gaelic	Phonetic
	S	
Sabbath	An Domnac	An Dhomnak
Saber	Claiom	Klhawm
Saddle	Diallaid	Dhiallaidh
Sailor	Marnealac	Marrneelhak
Saint	Naom	Nave
Salmon	Bradan	Bradhawn
Salt	Salann	Salann
Salute	Beannu Do	Beenu Dho
Same	Ceanna	Keena
Sand	Gaineam	Guhainam
Sardine	Seirdin	Sardeen
Satan	Diabal	Dhiabwal
Satin	Sroll	Srowll
Sauce	Anlann	Anlhann
Savage	Fiam	Fweeam
Scholar	Scolaire	Skollar
School	Scoil	Skool
Schoolboy	Garsun Scoil	Guharrsoon Skool
Schoolgirl	Gearrcaile Scoil	Guharrkall Skool
Scone	Toirtin	Thortheen
Scotchman	Albanac	Albwanak
Scout	Gasog	Guhsowg
Search	Cuardac	Kuarrdhak
Season	Seasur	Seesoor
Secret	Run	Roon
Seek	Loirgim	Llorrguheem
Sensation	Motu	Mothoo
Sentinel	Fear Faire	Feer Fwair
Serenade	Amran	Amrawn
Serpent	Natair Nime	Natair Neem
Shadow	Scat	Skawth
Shamrock	Seamrog	Shamrowguh
Shark	Miol Draide	Mol Dhrade
Sheep	Caora	Korra
Sheriff	Siriam	Shiriam

48

English	Gaelic	Phonetic
Shillelagh	Sillelagh	Shillalay
Shine	Snas	Snas
Shining	Snasta	Snastha
Ship	Long	Long
Short	Gearr	Guheerr
Shot	Plear	Pwleerr
Showy	Taispeantas	Thaispawnthas
Shrew	Bairseac	Bwawrsak
Shrimp	Ribe Roibeis	Ribe Robees
Sight	Radarc	Radhark
Silhouette	Scat	Skawth
Singer	Amranai	Amrawnai
Sir	Atair	Athair
Sitting	Seomra	Somrra
Sky	Speir	Spweer
Sleep	Codlad	Kodhlad
Sleepy	Codlatac	Kodhlathok
Slow	Mall	Mall
Small	Beag	Beg
Smart	Cliste	Klisthe
Smoke	Deatac	Dheethak
Smoky	Deataig	Dheethaguh
Snail	Seilmide	Seilmide
Snake	Atair Nime	Athair Neem
Snow	Sneacta	Snaktha
Society	Cumann	Kumann
Sock	Stoca	Sthoka
Soft	Bog	Bog
Soil	Cre	Kree
Soldier	Gorad	Guhoradh
Sole (fish)	Bonn	Bonn
Solid	Calad	Kalhadh
Solitary	Aonair	Aonairr
Solo	Amain	Amain
Song	Amran	Amrawn
Soothsayer	Easarlai	Eesarllai

49

English	Gaelic	Phonetic
South	Teas	Thees
Spade (cards)	Raman	Rrawman
Spaniel	Spaineor	Spwawneer
Sparkling	Dritleannac	Dhrithlenak
Spear	Slea	Slhay
Special	Speisialta	Spwesalhtha
Spice	Spiosra	Spweeosra
Spider	Daman	Dhamawn
Spindle	Fearsad	Feeresadh
Spiral	Cuardual	Kuardhule
Splinter	Scolp	Skolhpw
Sponge Cake	Maotciste	Mathkisth
Spoon	Spiunog	Spwoonowguh
Sport	Sugrad	Sooguhradh
Spot	Ball	Bwall
Sprinter	Coisi	Kosee
Spunky	Dana	Dhawnaw
Squad	Scata	Skatha
Square	Cearnog	Keernowguh
Squirrel	Iora Rua	Yora Roo
Stable	Stabla	Sthablha
Stag	Carria	Karria
Stagecoach	Coiste	Koisthe
Stallion	Stail	Sthal
Star	Realt	Reealth
Steed	Eac	Ak
Steel	Cruac	Krruak
Steward	Maor	Marr
Stile	Ceim	Keem
Stone	Cloc	Klhok
Stormy	Anaitiuil	Anatoolh
Stout (beverage)	Reamar	Reamar
Stove	Sorn	Sorrn
Stranger	Coicriocac	Koykreekak
Strawberry	Su Tallin	Soo Thalheen

English	Gaelic	Phonetic
Stream	Srut	Sruth
String	Sreang	Sranguh
Strip (noun)	Stiall	Sthile
Strong	Laidir	Laidhir
Stubborn	Ceann-Trean	Kan-Threen
Stud	Groig	Guhroiguh
Stupendous	Oll-Mor	Oll-Mor
Style	Mod	Mod
Sugar	Siucra	Swukra
Sun	Grian	Grian
Sunbeam	Gat Grian	Guhat Grian
Sunlight	Taitneam	Thathnam
Superior	Uactaran	Ooktharan
Superlative	Sar-Ceim	Sawr-Keem
Sweet	Milis	Milis
Sweetheart	Leannan	Lhenawn
Symphony	Comceol	Komkolh
Syrup	Sioroip	Sirup

T

English	Gaelic	Phonetic
Table	Bord	Bord
Tablecloth	Eadac Clair	Eedhak Klair
Tail	Eireaball	Eirebwall
Talent	Tallann	Thalhan
Talk	Caint	Kant
Tall	Ard	Awrd
Taskmaster	Maistir	Mawsther
Tea	Te	Thay
Teacher	Oide	Oide
Tempest	Anaite	Anaithe

English	Gaelic	Phonetic
Thanks	Buiocas	Bweekas
The	An	An
Thief	Gadi	Guhadi
Thing	Rud	Rud
Thoroughbred	Dea Poir	Dhe Pwoor
Thunder	Toirneac	Thornak
Tiger	Tiogar	Theeguhar
Timber	Admad	Adhmadh
Token	Comarta	Komartha
Top	Barr	Bwarr
Top Hat	Barr Hata	Bwarr Hatha
Torrent	Tuile	Thweelh
Tough	Rigin	Riguhin
Town	Baile	Bwalla
Toy	Breagan	Breeguhawn
Track	Lorg	Lhorguh
Tradition	Bealoidias	Beeloidhias
Traditional	Tradisiunta	Thradhisoontha
Trait	Lorg	Lhorguh
Traitor	Feallaire	Fweelhair
Traveler	Taistealai	Thaisthalhai
Treacle	Sioplas	Shopwlhas
Treasure	Ciste	Kisth
Tribute	Cain	Kawn
Trick	Cleas	Klees
Trifle (pudding)	Milseog	Milhsog
Trotting	Ar Sodar	Awr Sodar
Trout	Breac	Brake
Trumpet	Trumpa	Thrumpwa
Tune	Fonn	Fwon
Turnip	Turnap	Turnap
Turret	Binn	Bin
Twin	Leat-Cupla	Lheeth-Kupwlha
Typical	Samal-Crutac	Samal-Kruthak
Tyrant	Tioranac	Theerawnak

English	Gaelic	Phonetic
	U	
Ultimate	Deanac	Dheenak
Umpire	Moltoir	Molthoor
Union	Com-Ceangal	Kom-Kanguhalh
Unit	Aon	Aon
Unusual	Neam-Gnatac	Neem-Guhnathak
Up	Suas	Soos
Useful	Tairbeac	Thairbak
Utensil	Arcac	Arkak

English	Gaelic	Phonetic
	V	
Vagabond	Srataire	Srrathair
Vale	Gleann	Guhleen
Valiant	Calma	Kalhma
Valley	Gleann	Guhleen
Valor	Gaisce	Guhask
Valuable	Luacmar	Lhookmar
Very	An	Awn
Vetch	Pisean	Pwisawn
Victorious	Buac	Booak
Victory	Bua	Booa
Village	Baile	Bwalla
Vinegar	Fineagar	Fwinegar
Virtue	Suailce	Swawlke
Vision	Radarc	Radhark
Vixen	Sait Sionnaig	Sait Shonaguh
Vocal	Gotac	Guhothak
Voice	Gut	Guhuth
Volunteer (noun)	Oglac	Owguhlak
Vote	Bota	Boatha
Voyage	Iomram	Yomram

53

English	Gaelic	Phonetic
	W	
Wager	Geall	Guhall
Wagon	Trucail	Thrukail
Wake (to)	Duiseact	Dhweesakth
Wall	Falla	Fwalla
Wanderer	Fanai	Fwawnai
Warlock	Cogad Dual	Koguhadh Dhual
Warm	Te	The
Wasp	Beac Gabair	Bake Guhabair
Watchman	Fear Faire	Fweer Fwair
Water	Uisce	Whiska
Wealthy	Saibir	Saibir
Weaver	Fiodoir	Fweedhor
Welcome	Failte	Fwaltha
Well	Tobar	Thobawr
West	Tiar	Thiar
Wheat	Cruitneact	Krweethnakth
Whisker	Feasog	Fweasowguh
Whiskey	Uisce Beata	Whiska Bawtha
Whisper	Cogar	Koguhar
Whistle	Fead	Fweed
Whiting	Faoitin	Fwotheen
Whole	Iomlan	Yomlawn
Widow	Baintreac	Bwanthrrak
Widower	Baintreac Fir	Bwanthrrak Fweer
Wife	Ceile	Kaylhee
Wild	Fiain	Fwawn
Wildfire	Tind Dia	Thind Dhia
Willing	Toilteanac	Thoilthanak
Win	Buacaint	Buakanth
Wind	Gaot	Guhoth
Wine	Fion	Fweeon
Wise	Crionna	Kreena
Wish	Mian	Mian
Witch	Bandraoi	Bwandhra
Wizard	Draoi	Dhra

English	Gaelic	Phonetic
Wolf	Faol	Fwaol
Wonderful	Iontac	Younthak
Wool	Olann	Olan
Wooly	Olla	Olla
Work	Obair	Owbwair
Worthy	Fonta	Fwoontha
Writer	Scribneoir	Skrivener

Y

Yacht	Luam	Lhoom
Yard	Cleit	Kleeth
Yarn	Snat	Snath
Yes	Is Ea	Is Ee
Young	Og	Owg
Your	Do	Dho
Youthful	Og Oigeanta	Owg Oiguhantha

Z

Zealous	Dutractseag	Dhoothrakthseguh
Zenith	Forar	Fworar
Zest	Diograis	Dheeogras
Zigzag	Ar Fiar Sceo	Ar Fwar Sko
Zinc	Sionc	Shonk

Irish Terrier. Ch. Green Starr's Gold Strike, owned by Mrs. Frederick Sholes of Walton, New York. Bred by Dr. and Mrs. David G. Doane of Fort Belvoir, Virginia.

5. Specialized Listings

CARDINAL NUMBERS

As may be expected in this complex language, the numerals vary with the subject matter. In this selection, we give the basic number, the number with an associated noun, and the personal number.

English	Gaelic	Gaelic Number with Noun (horse, horses)	Phonetic
One	Aon	Aon Capall	An Kapall
Two	Do	D'a Capall	Dha Kapall
Three	Tri	Tri Capaill	Three Kapall
Four	Ceatair	Ceitre Capaill	Keethre Kapall
Five	Cuig	Cuig Capaill	Kweeguh Kapall
Six	Se	Se Capaill	See Kapall
Seven	Seact	Seact Gcapaill	Sekth Guhkapall
Eight	Oct	Oct Gcapaill	Oktha Guhkapall
Nine	Naoi	Naoi Gcapaill	Nay Guhkapall
Ten	Deic	Deic Gcapaill	Dhek Guhkapall
Eleven	Aon Deag	Aon Capall Deag	An Kapall Deguh
Twelve	Do Deag	Da Capall Deag	Dha Kapall Deguh
Thirteen	Tri Deag	Tri Capaill Deag	Three Kapall Deguh
Fourteen	Ceatair Deag	Ceitre Capaill Deag	Keethre Kapall Deguh
Fifteen	Cuig Deag	Cuig Capaill Deag	Kweeguh Kapall Deguh
Sixteen	Se Deag	Se Capaill Deag	See Kapall Deguh
Seventeen	Seact Deag	Seact Gcapaill Deag	Sekth Guhkapall Deguh

English	Gaelic	Gaelic Number with Noun (horse, horses)	Phonetic
Eighteen	Oct Deag	Oct Gcapaill Deag	Okth Guhkapall Deguh
Nineteen	Naoi Deag	Naoi Gcapaill Deag	Nay Guhkapall Deguh
Twenty	Fice	Fice Capall	Fwice Kapall
Thirty	Trioca	Trioca Capall	Threooka Kapall
Forty	Daicead	Daicead Capall	Dhaikad Kapall
Fifty	Caoga	Caoga Capall	Kaguha Kapall
Sixty	Seasca	Seasca Capall	Seska Kapall
Seventy	Seatto	Seatto Capall	Setto Kapall

When the numerals apply to persons, the personal number must be used.

English	Gaelic	Phonetic
One	Duine	Dhween
Two	Beirt	Berth
Three	Triur	Threeoor
Four	Ceatrar	Kathrar
Five	Cuigear	Kweeguhar
Six	Seisear	Seseer
Seven	Seactar	Sekthar
Eight	Octar	Okthar
Nine	Naonur	Nonoor
Ten	Deicniur	Dheknoor

ORDINAL NUMBERS

English	Gaelic	Phonetic
The First Horse	An Cead Capall	An Kad Kapall
The Second Horse	An Dou Capall	An Dhou Kapall
The Third Horse	An Triu Capall	An Threeoo Kapall
The Fourth Horse	An Ceatru Capall	An Kathroo Kapall
The Fifth Horse	An Cuigiu Capall	An Kweeguh Kapall
The Sixth Horse	An Seu Capall	An Seeoo Kapall
The Seventh Horse	An Seactu Capall	An Sekthoo Kapall
The Eighth Horse	An T-octu Capall	An Thokthoo Kapall
The Ninth Horse	An Naou Capall	An Noo Kapall
The Tenth Horse	An Deiciu Capall	An Dhekoo Kapall
The Eleventh Horse	An T-aonu Capall	An Thonoo Kapall
The Fortieth Horse	Deag	Deguh
The Forty First Horse	An Daiceadu Capall	An Daykadoo Kapall
	An T-aonu Capall is	An Thonoo Kapall is
The One Hundredth	Daicead	Dhaykod
Horse	An Ceadu Capall	An Kadoo Kapall
The One Hundred		
and First Horse	An T-aonu Capall	An Thonoo Kapall Kad
	Cead	

THE FOUR SEASONS

English	Gaelic	Phonetic
The Spring	Awn Thearrak	An Tearrac
The Summer	Awn Samrradh	An Samrad
The Autumn	Awn Fwomarr	An Fomar
The Winter	Awn Guhemredh	An Geimread

59

THE MONTHS

English	Gaelic	Phonetic
January	Eanair	Eanairr
February	Feabra	Fwebrra
March	Marta	Martha
April	Aibrean	Abran
May	Bealtaine	Belthan
June	Meiteam	Metham
July	Luil	Llweel
August	Lunasa	Lloonasa
September	Mean Fomair	Mean Fwomair
October	Deiread Fomair	Dheread Fwomair
November	Samain	Saman
December*	Mi Nollag	My Nollaguh

THE DAYS OF THE WEEK

English	Gaelic	Phonetic
Sunday	An Domnac	Awn Dhomnak
Monday	An Luan	Awn Llooan
Tuesday	An Mairt	Awn Mairth
Wednesday	An Ceadaoin	Awn Kadoin
Thursday	An Dardaoin	Awn Dharrdhoin
Friday	An Aoine	Awn Aoine
Saturday	An Satarn	Awn Satharrn

*Translated "Month of the Birth of Christ"

OTHER WORDS RELATING TO TIME

English	Gaelic	Phonetic
Afternoon	Iaronoin	Yarronown
Almanac	Feilire	Fweelhir
Calendar	Feilire	Fweelhir
Day	La	Law
Evening	Tratnona	Thrawthnowna
Ever	Riam	Ryam
Everlasting	Siorbuan	Shorboon
Midday	Meanlae	Mawnlae
Midnight	Meanoice	Mawnoees
Month	Mi	Mee
Moon	Re	Ree
Morning	Maidean	Maidhan
Never	Riam	Ryam
New	Nua	Nua
New Year	Nua Bliam	Nua Blhyam
Night	Oice	Oees
Noon	Meanlae	Mawnlae
Old	Aosta	Aostha
Once	Aon Uair Amain	Aon Ooarr Aman
Overdue	Tar Am	Thar Am
Punctual	Poncuil	Pwonkweel
Sunrise	Eiri Greme	Eree Guhreem
Sunset	Lui Grian	Lhui Guhrryan
Thereafter	Na Diaid	Na Dhiaidh
Time	Aimsir	Amsirr
Timely	Tratuil	Thrathweelh
Today	Inniu	Inwee
Tomorrow	Amarac	Amarrak
Tonight	Anoct	Anokth
Unpunctual	Mi-Poncuil	Mi-Pwonkweel
Until	Go	Go
Untimely	Antratac	Anthrawthak
When	An Uair	Awn Wair
Year	Bliam	Blhyam
Yesterday	An La Inne	Awn Law Inee
Yet	Fos	Fwows

61

TREES, SHRUBS, AND RELATED TERMS

English	Gaelic	Phonetic
Acorn	Cno Darac	Konow Dharrak
Alder	Fearna	Fweerrna
Apple	Ull	Oolh
Arbutus	Caitne	Kaithne
Ash	Fuinseog	Fweenseoguh
Aspen	Crann Creata	Krrann Kreetha
Beech	Fea-Bile	Fwaw-Bilhe
Birch	Beit	Beeth
Botany	Luibeola	Lhweebeolha
Bough	Geag	Guheaguh
Bramble	Dris	Drees
Bush	Tor	Thor
Chestnut	Geanmeno	Guhanmeno
Cypress	Crann Cufair	Kran Koofwair
Elder	Crann Troim	Kran Throim
Elm	Leaman	Lheemawn
Fig Tree	Crann Fige	Kran Fwiguh
Fir	Giuis	Guhwees
Foliage	Duilliur	Dhweelhurr
Forest	Foraois	Fworais
Grove	Garran	Guharrawn
Hawthorn	Sceac	Skaik
Hazel	Coll	Koll
Hedge	Fal	Fwal
Hemlock	Milmear	Milmeerr
Holly	Cuileann	Kweelan
Laburnum	Labran	Lhabrawn
Larch	Learog	Lherowguh
Laurel	Labras	Lhabrras
Leaf	Duille	Dhweel
Maple	Crann Mailp	Kran Mailpw
Mountain Ash	Caortann	Korrthan
Oak	Dair	Dhair
Olive Tree	Crann Ola	Kran Olha
Orchard	Ablord	Ablhordh
Palm	Pailm	Pwalhm

62

English	Gaelic	Phonetic
Pine	Giuis	Guhwees
Poplar	Crann Creata	Kran Kreetha
Shrub	Tor	Thor
Sloe Tree	Dreagean Dub	Dhragan Dhub
Spruce	Giuis	Guhwees
Sycamore	Crann Ban	Kran Bwawn
Sylvan	Craobac	Krabwak
Thorn	Dealg	Dhelhguh
Timber	Admad	Adhmadh
Tree	Crann	Kran
Twig	Slat	Slhath
Walnut	Gall-Gno	Guhall-Guhnow
Willow	Saileac	Sailhak
Yew	Iur	Eeurr

JEWELS AND JEWELRY

Beads	Paidrin	Pawhrreen
Bracelet	Braislead	Brraslhed
Brooch	Dealg	Dhalhguh
Diamond	Diomant	Dheemanth
Emerald	Cloc Smearagard	Klok Smeerraguhardh
Gem	Geam	Guheem
Gold	Or	Owrr
Jewel	Seoid	Shodh
Ornament	Ornaid	Orrnawd
Pearl	Pearla	Pweerrlha
Precious	Luacmar	Lhooakmarr
Quartz	Grian Cloc	Guhrrian Klhok
Ruby	Flanncloc	Fwlhanklhok
Silver	Airgead	Airrguhadh
Silversmith	Gaba Geal	Guhbwa Guhalh
Solitaire	Aonair	Aonairr
Sterling	Dilis	Dheelhis
Stone	Cloc	Klhok
Trinket	Ailleagan	Awlheeguhan

63

FLOWERS AND RELATED TERMS

English	Gaelic	Phonetic
Bloom	Blat	Blhawth
Blossom	Blat	Blhawth
Buttercup	Cam	Kam
Clover	Seamar	Seemarr
Cowslip	Bobleact	Bowblhakth
Daffodil	Blat Cromcinn	Blhawth Krromkin
Daisy	Nomin	Nowmeen
Dandelion	Caisearban	Kaseerbwawn
Fern	Raitneac	Rraithnak
Flower	Blat	Blhawth
Furze	Aiteann	Aithean
Garden	Garrai	Guharree
Garland	Fleasc	Fwlhask
Gorse	Aiteann	Aithean
Grass	Fear	Fweer
Heath	Fraoc Min	Fwraok Meen
Heather	Fraoc Min	Fwraok Meen
Hyacinth	Bu	Boo
Lilac	Dreasan	Dhrreesawn
Lily	Lil	Lhilh
Myrtle	Roideog	Rroidhoguh
Primrose	Samaircin	Samairkin
Rose	Ros	Rows
Shamrock	Seamrog	Shamrowguh
Sprig	Beangan	Beanguhan
Stem	Gas	Guhas
Thistle	Feocadan	Fweekadhawn
Thyme	Tim	Theem
Verdure	Fasra	Fwawsrra
Vine	Finium	Fweenloom
Violet	Salcuac	Salhkook
Wall Fern	Sceam	Skeem
Woodbine	Taiteileann	Thawtheethan
Wreath	Fleasc	Fwleesk

COLORS

English	Gaelic	Phonetic
Blue	Gorm	Guhorrm
Brown	Donn	Dhon
Crimson	Dearg	Dheerguh
Emerald	Uaine	Wain
Golden	Orga	Oorrguha
Gray	Liat	Lhiath
Green	Uaine	Wain
Lavender	Lus Liat	Lhus Lhiath
Mottled	Breac	Brrake
Orange	Odarbui	Oodharbwee
Purple	Corcora	Korrkorra
Red	Dearg	Dheerguh
Roan	Donn	Dhon
Rust	Meirg	Merrguh
Saffron	Croc	Krroke
Scarlet	Cro Dearg	Krro Dheerguh
Speckled	Breac	Brrake
Tan	Cron	Krron
Tint	Sceo	Skyo
Yellow	Bui	Bwee

BIRDS

English	Gaelic	Phonetic
Birds	Ean	Een
Blackbird	Lon	Lhon
Crow	Preacan	Pwrrakawn
Cuckoo	Cuac	Kooak
Curlew	Crotac	Krrothak
Dove	Colur	Kolhoor
Drake	Bardal	Bwawdhalh
Duck	Laca	Llaka

English	Gaelic	Phonetic
Falcon	Seabac	Seebhak
Gannet	Gainead	Guhaineedh
Goldfinch	Lasair Coil	Llasair Kolh
Goose	Ge	Guhee
Grouse	Cearc Fraoig	Karrk Fwrraguh
Gull	Faoilean	Fwoilheen
Hawk	Seabac	Seebwak
Heron	Corr	Korr
Jackdaw	Cag	Kaguh
Lapwing	Pilbin	Pwilhbeen
Lark	Fuiseog	Fwoosoguh
Magpie	Snag Breac	Snaguh Brraik
Mallard	Bardal	Bwawdhalh
Ostrich	Strutac	Sthrroothak
Parrot	Piorroid	Pwerrowdh
Partridge	Piotraisc	Pwithrrask
Peacock	Peacog	Pweekaguh
Pee-Wit	Pilbin	Pwilhbeen
Petrel	Guardal	Guharrdhalh
Pheasant	Feasun	Fweasun
Pigeon	Colur	Kolhoor
Plover	Feadog	Fweedhoguh
Poultry	Eanlaite Ti	Eenlhaith Thy
Quail	Traona	Thrrona
Raven	Fiac Dub	Fwiak Dubh
Redwing	Siocan	Showkawn
Robin	Spideog	Spwidhoguh
Rook	Preacan	Pwrrakawn
Sandpiper	Gobadan	Guhobwadhawn
Seagull	Faoilean	Fwailhan
Skylark	Fuiseog	Fweesoguh
Sparrow	Gealban	Guheelhbwan
Sparrow-Hawk	Seabac Rua	Seebwak Roo
Stork	Corr	Korr
Swan	Eala	Eelha
Thrush	Smolac	Smowlhak

English	Gaelic	Phonetic
Turkey	Cearc Francac	Kerrk Fwrrankak
Vulture	Badb	Bwad
Wing	Sciatan	Skeethawn
Woodcock	Creabar	Kreebarr
Wood-pigeon	Colur	Kolhoor
Wren	Dreoilin	Dhrrolhin

FAMILY RELATIONSHIPS

English	Gaelic	Phonetic
Aunt	Aintin	Awnthin
Brother	Deartair	Dheerrthawrr
Child	Leanb	Lheen
Children	Leanai	Lheenay
Cousin	Colceatai	Kolhkeetha
Daughter	Mion	Myon
Father	Atair	Athar
Grandchild	Garmac	Guharrmak
Granddam	Sean-Matair	Shawn-Matharr
Grandfather	Sean-Atair	Shawn-Atharr
Grandmother	Sean-Matair	Shawn-Matharr
Grandsire	Sean-Atair	Shawn-Atharr
Grandson	Mac Mic	Mak Mik
Greatgrandfather	Sin-Seanatair	Shin-Shawnatharr
Greatgrandmother	Sin-Seanmatair	Shin-Shawnmatharr
Husband	Fearceile	Fweerkeelh
Mother	Matair	Matharr
Sire	Atair	Atharr
Sister	Deirfuir	Dheerfwerr
Son	Buacaill	Bookal
Son-in-law	Cliamain	Klhyman
Spouse	Ceile	Kaylhee
Uncle	Uncal	Unkalh
Widow	Baintreac	Bwanthrrak
Widower	Baintreac Fir	Bwanthrrak Fweer
Wife	Ceile	Kaylhee

67

Clowning around with an Airedale Terrier.

6. Irish and Scottish Place-Names as Names for Kennels

Many Irish and Scottish place-names are poetic and would provide attractive names for kennels. Some, such as Dunleary and Tralee, are in actual use. Some breeder could use the fanciful Scottish name Brigadoon. However, if you wish to have your kennel name registered with The American Kennel Club and thereby acquire a protection similar to that of a United States copyright but to a limited degree, then you may have trouble convincing the AKC that it should not oppose the use of existing place-names as kennel names. It was for this reason that we devised a Gaelic composite word "Baileglas" or Town of the Green Plain, as our own kennel name. No great number of applications for name registry are received by the AKC and thousands of kennel names seem to thrive in unregistered bliss. The fact that we have not applied for registration of the name "Baileglas" is not meant to downgrade the prestige which may surround such registry.

Most Scottish place-names have a degree of Gaelic origin. The counties, thirty-three in number, are the largest geographical divisions. Their names are:

Aberdeen	Lanark
Angus (also known as Forfar)	Midlothian
Argyll	Moray
Banff	Nairn
Berwick	Orkney
Bute	Peebles
Caithness	Perth
Dunbarton	Ross and Cromarty
Dumfries	Roxburge
East Lothian	Selkirk
Fife	Shetland
Inverness	Stirling
Kincardine	Sutherland
Kinross	West Lothian
Kirkcudbright	Wigtown

It is unlikely that any fancier would want to name a kennel after a county bearing the dual name of Ross and Cromarty but either of the two names would be usable. Also, while East Lothian, Midlothian, and West Lothian are doubtful choices, Lothian would be a good choice.

Other place-names, including cities and geographical locations, are appropriate. The cities are officially known as burghs and their names are: Glasgow, the largest, Edinburgh (pronounced Edinburra), the capital, and, in their descending order of population-size, Aberdeen, Dundee, Paisley, Greenock, Motherwell, Kirkaldy, Coatbridge, and Dunfermline.

Geographical points with attractive names include Arran, Hebrides, Clyde, Lorne, Dornock, Tay, Mull of Galloway, Linnhe, Ben Nevis, Ben Macdhui, Ochil, Flintry, Merrick, Cairnsmore, Cheviot, Loch Lomond, Loch Katrine, Tweed, Spay, and Dee. (You would probably not want to name your kennel Spay unless you were to engage in that specialty.)

The largest geographical areas of Ireland are the provinces, four in number, which Irish legend has termed "The Four Green Fields"— namely, the provinces of Ulster, of which the largest city is Belfast; Connaught, of which the largest city is Galway; Leinster, of which the largest city is Dublin; and Munster, of which the largest city is Cork. Of these, Ulster was formerly the most patriotic, Leinster was the mainstay of the so-called Danes, Munster flaunts the most pronounced brogue, and Connaught is always associated with the despot-invader Oliver Cromwell, of whom it is said, "He drove the Irish to hell or Connaught." And it is also observed that Cromwell is now deceased and no one knows where he went but he has not been seen in Connaught.

The counties are the geographical divisions next in size. There are thirty-two—twenty-six in the Republic of Ireland and six in Northern Ireland, that separated and troublesome member of the British Empire. Of the nine counties in Ulster, the following three are in the Republic of Ireland:

English Name	Gaelic Name	Gaelic Meaning
Donegal	Dun Nan Goll	The Fortress of the Foreigners
Cavan	An Cabain	The Hollow Place
Monaghan	Muineacan	Little Hills

The following six counties of Ulster are in Northern Ireland:

English Name	Gaelic Name	Gaelic Meaning
Antrim	Aontroma	Elder Tree
Down	Duin	A Fort
Armagh	Ard Maca	Macha's Height
Derry	Doire	Oak Grove
Tyrone	Tir Eogain	Owen's Glen
Fermanagh	Fear Manac	

The other twenty-three counties in the Republic of Ireland, listed by provinces, are:

English Name	Leinster Gaelic Name	Gaelic Meaning
Dublin	Ata Cliat	Hurdle-Ford
Wicklow	Cill Mantan	Church of Saint Mantan
Wexford	Loc Garman	Lake of Garman
Kilkenny	Cill Cainnig	Canice's Church
Carlow	Ceatarlac	Fourfold Lake
Kildare	Cill Dara	Church of the Oak
Laois	Laoigis	The Fort of Laoghis
Offaly	Uab Failge	
Westmeath	Na Hiarmroe	
Longford	Longport	Fortress
Meath	Na Mide	
Louth	Lugbard	

English Name	*Munster* *Gaelic Name*	*Gaelic Meaning*
Cork	Corcaig	Marshy Place
Kerry	Ciarraige	
Limerick	Luimneac	Bare Spot
Clare	An Clair	
Tipperary	Tiobrad Arann	The Well of Ara
Waterford	Port Lairge	The Port of Lairge
	Connaught	
Galway	Gaillim	Gailleamh's Place
Mayo	Muigeo	
Sligo	Sligeac	The Shelly River
Leitrim	Liatdroma	
Roscommon	Ros Comain	Coeman's Wood

Many of the place-names in Ireland which would serve well as names for kennels are associated with the animals of Ireland, which are, to a large degree, different from those of the rest of Europe because Ireland became separated from England long before England became separated from the Continent. (If there were to be a lowering of the seas by only three hundred feet, both England and Ireland would be reunited to Europe.)

The earlier separation of Ireland from the Continent results in such differences that neither the weasel nor the mole are found in Ireland. Similarly, England has four breeds of mice while Ireland has only two. And, as we are constantly reminded, Ireland is devoid of snakes. Proof that Scotland and Ireland were joined in the vicinity of the Giant's Causeway after Irish land was separated from English, lies in the fact that the Irish hare is the same as the Scottish hare and unlike that of England. The same comments are true in the variations of arboreal life. The rowan tree, for example, is indigenous to Ireland and Scotland but not to England.

Keeping in mind this background of the nature of poetic small-town names associated with animal life and arboreal life in Ireland and Scotland, any of the following are appropriate for a kennel:

English Name	*Gaelic Name*	*Gaelic Meaning*
The Curragh	Currac Cill Dara	The Racecourse of Kildare
Castlepollard	Cionn Torc	The Hill of the Boars
Foynes	Faing	The Raven

English Name	*Gaelic Name*	*Gaelic Meaning*
Swinford	Beat Ata Na Muice	Ford-mouth of the Pigs
Portnabo	Port Nabo	Cow's Bay
Limavady	Leim a Madaid	The Dog's Leap
Newry	Lubar Cinn Traga	Strand-head Yew Tree
Derry	Doire	Oak Grove
Lucan	Leamcan	Marsh Mallow Land
Woodenbridge	Garran an Gablain	The Shrubbery of the River Fork
New Ross	Ros Mic Treoin	The Wood of the Son of Tream
Ferns	Fearna	The Alder Trees
Bagenalstown	Muine Bheag	Little Shrubbery
Kildare	Cill Dara	The Church of the Oak
Edenderry	Eadan Doire	Oakwood Hill-brow
Edgeworthstown	Meatas Truim	Elder Tree Fruit
Trim	Baile Ata Truim	Town of Elder Tree Ford
Cork	Corkaig	A Marsh
Youghal	Eocaill	Yew Wood
Rosscarbery	Ros Cairbre	Carberry Wood
Ballingeary	Beal Ata an Gaortaig	Ford of the River Shrubbery
Glenbeigh	Gleann Beite	Birch Tree Glen
Ballybunion	Baile an Buinneanaig	The Town of the Sapling
Clonmel	Cluain Meala	Honey Meadow
Roscrea	Ros Cre	Crea's Wood
Cahir	Catair Duin Lascaig	Fortress of the Fish-Abounding Dun
Portumna	Port Omna	Oak Harbor
Ballaghaderreen	Bealac a Doirin	The Road of the Little Oak Wood
Ballybay	Beal Ata Beite	Ford-Mouth of the Birch
Carrickmacross	Carraig Macaire Ros	The Rock of the Wooded Plain
Ballymoney	Baile Muine	The Town of the Shrubbery
Coleraine	Cuil Ratain	Ferry Corner
Magherafelt	Macaire Fiogaid	Rushy Plain

Scottish Collie, American and Bermudian Ch. Wickmere Rapunzel, owned by Mrs. George H. Roos, Jr., Wickmere Collies, Fairfax, Virginia.

Border Terrier, Ch. Rob Roys Buckler, owned by Marian duPont Scott and handled by Damara Bolte.

8. Gaelic Feminine Names

As noted earlier, the record of Gaelic feminine names is extensive because for many centuries Ireland has, to a marked degree, had a matriarchal society. Naturally, this is true of Scotland to some extent, also. Modern examples of women of authority and leadership include the Countess Markiewicz, one of the two commandants of the Republican forces in Saint Stephen's Green during the Easter Rising of 1916, and Anna Parnell, who served as the president of the effective Ladies' Land League in 1881. A familiar older name is that of Grainne O'Malley, "Queen of the Seas," who established a large fleet of merchant ships operating from Aichill Island. But the poetic old Gaelic names are those which you will wish to bestow upon the dogs of Ireland and Scotland.

When we recall old Gaelic feminine names, the first in our thoughts are Medb (Maeve), Deirdre, and Emer. "Deirdre of the Sorrows" was the tragic friend of the Sons of Usnach, celebrated in plays by John Millington Synge and William Butler Yeats and in stories by James Stephens, Frank O'Connor, and many others. And Emer was the betrothed of Cuchulain.

There are fewer old Gaelic feminine names than masculine, but because of the Gaels' extraordinary inventiveness with words, there is no dearth of names for female dogs.

Gaelic   *Phonetic*

A

Gaelic	Phonetic	
Achlene	Okleen	A sister of Saint Patrick
Agata	Agawta	The Good
Aigneis	Awgnas	The Pure
Ailbhe	Alvi	Olive
Ailis	Aylis	The Truthful
Aine	Anne	From the Hebrew
Aingeal	Angawl	The Angel
Annabla	Anabel	Norman - Irish

Gaelic	*Phonetic*	
	B	
Bab	Babe	A pet name
Bagha	Bee	Seventh century daughter of an Irish King; she founded a monastery in Cumberland, Scotland
Baine	Bawn	A daughter of the king of the Picts
Bairbre	Barbara	Patron saint of architects and engineers
Beara	Bawra	A queen of ancient Ireland
Bebhinn	Bevin (Vivian)	The mother of Brian Boroimbh
Bevin	Bevin	The melodious
Blath	Flora	A virgin saith
Boann	Bow-an	The River Goddess
Breathigrend	Burrteegrend	A queen of ancient Ireland
Brenda	Brenda	The Raven
Brigit	Breejit	The Poetry Goddess
Bridget	Breedhit	Fifth century saint; "Mary of the Gael"
Bryna	Bwreena	The Strong
	C	
Caitlin	Kateleen	The Pure
Canair	Konawr	Fifth century advocate of women's lib
Caoilfhionn	Keelin	"Slender and Fair"
Carthann	Kawthan	The mother of Niall, q.v.
Ceara	Kawra	The Spear
Ciar	Keara	A saint of Tipperary
Ciarnat	Kyarnat	Concubine of Cormac, q.v.
Clare	Klair	Clear, bright

Gaelic	*Phonetic*	
Clodagh	Klodda	A river in Tipperary, increasing in popularity as a name for girls
Comghan	Kuman	Eighth century, sister of Ceallach (Kelly), a king of Leinster
Conchessa	Konchessa	The mother of Saint Patrick
Cristin	Khristeen	A Christian

D

Dairine	Dawreen	A daughter of Tuathail, q.v.
Darenca	Darenka	A sister of Saint Patrick
Dearbhail	Derval	True Desire
Deirdre	Daredra	"Of the Sorrows"; the friend of the Sons of Usnach
Doreen	Doreen	The Gloomy
Dymphna	Demfna	A king's daughter from the County Monaghan; the patron saint of the deranged

E

Earnait	Ernet	"Knowing"
Edain	Eedawn	A queen of the Tuatha DeDanann
Edana	Eedana	Received the convent veil from Saint Patrick
Eibhilin	Evelean	"Sunlight"
Eire	Eyera	A queen of the DeDananns
Eistir	Esther	From the Hebrew
Emer	Ever	The beauteous sweetheart of Cuchulain
Ena	Eena	The Fiery
Etaoin	Aideen	A saint in Connacht
Ethne	Eethinee	"Sweet kernel of a nut"

Gaelic	*Phonetic*	
	F	
Fainche	Fanny	A saintly virgin in Rossary
Fedelm	Feedelim	A queen of ancient Ireland
Fionnuala	Finola	"Fair shoulder"
Fithir	Fithirr	A daughter of Tuathail, q.v.
Flanna	Flanna	The Red-haired
	G	
Gemma	Gemma	A gem
Ghleanna	Glenna	The Lady of the Glen
Gobnait	Gobnawt	Irish for Deborah; famous saint from Cork
Gormlaith	Gurumla	A queen of ancient Ireland
Grainne	Granya	A sea-queen of the sixteenth century
	I	
Ita	Eta	Sixth Century; "Foster Mother of the Saints of Ireland"
	K	
Kentigerna	Kentigerna	A sister of Ceallach (Kelly), King of Leinster
Kyna	Kyna	The Wise
	L	
Lasairiona	Lassarina	"Flaming Wine"
Lendabair	Lendabawn	A queen of ancient Ireland
Lil	Lily	Nickname for Elizabeth
Lupida	Loopida	A sister of Saint Patrick

Gaelic	*Phonetic*	
	M	
Macha	Makka	Second century B.C.; first Milesian queen of Ireland
Madailein	Madeline	After Saint Mary Magdalen
Maureen	Maureen	Little Mary
Mealla	Mella	Name of Irish holy women
Medb	Maeve	The Warrior Queen of Connaught
Meghan	Meegan	The Mighty
Mide	Meeda	"Dear Ita"
Mong	Monga	A queen of ancient Ireland
Muireann	Morrin	"Of the long hair"
Myrna	Meerna	The Gentle
	N	
Nainsi	Nancy	Variant of Anne
Neala	Neela	The Champion
Nora	Nora	The Honored One
	O	
Ona	Owna	The Lone
Orfhlaith	Orla	"Golden Lady"
Orna	Awrna	The Olive
	P	
Patricia	Patrisha	After Princess Patricia of Connaught
Philomena	Philomena	Friend, power
Proinnseas	Froynsas	Feminine of Francis

Gaelic	*Phonetic*	

R

Rathnait	Ranna	Patron saint of Kilkenny
Richael	Richile	A virgin saint
Riognach	Reena	Saint Regina, virgin
Rois	Rose	Hros or horse

S

Sabia	Saybia	A queen of ancient Ireland
Sadhbh	Sive	"Goodness"
Saraid	Sayrawd	A queen of ancient Ireland
Seaslait	Sharlott	Feminine of Charles
Scota	Skowta	Pharoah's daughter after whom Scotia was named
Segresia	Saygraysia	A sister of Saint Patrick
Seosaimhin	Josefeen	Modern feminine of Joseph
Sheila	Sheela	The near-sighted
Sibeal	Shibeel	The Prophetess
Sinead	Janet	From Johanna
Sorcha	Sorrcha	The Bright
Susanna	Susanna	Lily - grace

T

Tullia	Toolia	The Quiet

U

Uallach	Oo-a-lak	A chief ancient poetess
Una	Oona	An Irish form of Agnes
Ursula	Ursula	Latin for Little Bear

V

Vanessa	Vanessa	Anagram by Dean Swift

Bearded Collie. *Photo by Jo Parker.*

Greyhound, Ch. Iveragh Captain Midnite of Cebar, bred by Deborah C. Littleton and owned by Susan Oglebay, Silver Spring, Maryland. Shown here as Best of Winners, handled by Julia Cupurdija under Colonel Wallace Pede.

9. Gaelic Masculine Names

When masculine names for dogs are considered, the first which comes to mind is that of Cuchulain (or Cu Cullan), the legendary hero who derived the prefix of his name, "Cu," meaning Hound, from a youthful adventure. Originally Cuchulain's name was Setanta. One day, as he approaced the home of a blacksmith named Cullan, Setanta thought, in error, that he was being attacked by the hound of the house, which he quickly killed. In remorse, Setanta said to Cullan, "I shall henceforth be your Hound, O Cullan." And from then on he was known as Cu Cullan, or Cuchulain, the Hound of Cullan.

The word "Cu" is associated with many Gaelic first names and surnames, An example is MacCumara (now McNamara) or Hound of the Sea. Another example is Cu Roi Mac Daire, the legendary hero at the fall of Dind Rig, as recounted in the Tain. Such examples testify to the close psychic relationship which the Gaels have always had with animals, especially dogs and cattle.

In the General Post Office on O'Connell Street in Baile Atha Cliath (Dublin) there is a half-size statue of Cuchulain in memory of Padraeg Pearse, James Connolly, and the others who held the building as their army headquarters during the Rising of Easter Monday 1916. The Rising, while unsuccessful, led to the freedom of what is now the Republic of Ireland. A foot of the bronze figure is worn smooth by thousands of patriot hands, and, who knows, perhaps by an equal number of dog lovers responding to the inspiration of the Hound of Cullan.

> ...but they say that every woman
> loves the Cu.
>
> —Deirdre—James Stephens

There is no scarcity of Gaelic masculine names and thousands could be cited. The names which we have selected have varying significance —some heroic, others referring to saints and scholars, others to personal qualities, and still others such as Colin and Conway referring to dogs exactly. The names listed cover many centuries but are concentrated in the fifth, sixth, and seventh centuries, A.D.

83

Gaelic	Phonetic	
	A	
Abban	Abban	Famous Leinster saint of the sixth century
Adamnan	Adamnawn	Abbot of Iona and scholar
Aengus	Aingus	Warrior who killed Ceallach, son of Cormac, q.v.
Aguistin	Awgusteen	"Venerable"
Aiden	Ayden	The fiery one
Ailbhe	Alve	Fifth century abbot who built The Cathedral at Emly in the County of Tipperary
Ailfrid	Alfred	Norman, Alfred the Great
Ailill	Alill	Third husband of Queen Medb, q.v.
Ailin	Allen	Noble
Alroy	Alroo	The red-headed
Alsander	Alsander	Irish of Alexander
Amergin	Amerghin	A Milesian poet
Amhlaoibh	Olav	Introduced by the Norsemen
Arlen	Arlin	The truthful one
Art	Art	Ancient Irish "Stone"
	B	
Bainin	Bawneen	The white one
Baird	Bawrd	A writer and singer of ballads
Balor	Balor	A chief of the Fomorians
Beagan	Byngawn	A little one
Bearach	Barry	Spear, javelin
Benen	Bawnen	Fifth century, the second bishop of Armagh and a friend of Saint Patrick

84

Gaelic   *Phonetic*

Bernard	Bernard	Bear-like
Bhailintin	Valentine	Strong, healthy
Blaine	Blayn	The lean one
Blair	Blair	Man of the fields
Boyne	Boin	The River Boyne, the Battle of Boyne, 1690
Brady	Braydee	A man of spirit
Bran	Bran	A Hound of Fionn's men
Breas	Brees	A chief of the DeDananns
Brendan	Brendan	Voyager and saint who may have discovered America before Columbus or Ericson
Brian	Breeun	Brother of Niall, q.v.
Bricriu	Breekroo	The Bitter-tongued
Bronach	Bronak	Sixth century; the Saint of the Bronze Bell
Buadhach	Booaw	Victory
Buite	Bwuich	Sixth century; founded Abbey of Monasterboice

C

Cairbre	Kaibr	An ancient Irish poet
Calbhach	Kalvaw	"The Bald"
Calporn	Kalpawn	The Father of Saint Patrick
Caolan	Keelan	"The Cool"
Carbraw	Karbraw	An ancient Leinster chief
Carlin	Karlen	A champion
Carney	Karnee	A victor
Casey	Kaysee	A good, all-around soldier
Cassidy	Kassidee	The clever one
Cathair	Kare	O'Doherty and O'Galagher name

Gaelic	Phonetic	
Cathal	Kahal	The most famous Italian Irish saint after whom the city of San Cataldo is named
Cathfa		A famous poet
Cavan	Kaffa	The handsome one
Ceallach	Kavan	"War, strife"
Ceannfaelad	Kella Karnfalawda	The seventh century Irish commander who invaded Wales
Cearbhall		Irish for Charles
Cearnac	Karroll	The Victorious
Cian	Karnak	An ancient poet
Cianan	Keeawn	The Bishop of Duleek
Cimbaoth	Keenan Kimbayth	A king, husband of Macha, q.v.
Cleary		A scholar
Cluny	Kleeree	A worker in the field
Cobtach	Kloonee	A grandson of Ugani, q.v.
Coilcan	Kobtok	"Whelp"
Colcu	Kolin Kolkoo	A chief professor of Clonmacnois
Colin		A pup or cub
Colla	Kowlin	Ancient Irish
Comgall	Kolla Komgall	The abbott of Benchor Ulaid
Comhghan		"Twin"
Conaire	Kowan	A king at the time of Christ
Conchobar	Konnor Kun-a-hoor	A king of Ulaid (Ulster) at the time of Christ
Conlon		A hero
Conn	Konlon Konn	Hero of the Hundred Battles, a grandson of Tuathail, q.v.
Connall	Konawl	A warrior (hound)

Gaelic	*Phonetic*	
Connera	Kunnora	Sixth century; patron saint of Irish seamen
Connlaoi	Konlee	"Prudent Fire"
Conway	Konway	The Hound of the Plain
Corcoran	Korkoran	The Red-faced
Cormac	Kormak	Third century king of Ireland; grandson of Conn
Cowan	Kowan	A twin
Coyle	Koyl	A foot-soldier
Craftine	Krafteen	A celebrated ancient harpist
Creidne	Kreena	A great DeDanann artificer
Crimthann	Krimthawn	A king who was famous for expeditions; uncle of Niall, q.v.
Crom	Krom	An idol destroyed by Saint Patrick
Cronan	Kronan	Seventh century; ancestor of John Carroll, first bishop of the United States
Cuain	Kooawn	Eleventh century poet
Cuchulain	Koohullawn	From cu, the word for Hound; named for mistakenly killing one when a boy; the greatest of the legendary Irish heroes
Cummian	Koomian	A scholar, "The Tall"
Curran	Kurran	A champion

D

Dagda	Dagda	A leader of the DeDananns
Daibheid	David	Saint David

Gaelic	*Phonetic*	
Damhnaic	Domnik	Saint Dominick
Dathi	Dawthee	A nephew of Niall, q.v.
Darby	Dawbee	A free man
Diancecht	Donnka	A famous Druid physician
Diarmuid	Dermod	Saint Jeremiah
Domnoc	Domnok	Introduced bees and honey
Donal	Donall	"World-mighty"
Donnchad	Dunukha	A brother of Saint Patrick
Dorbene	Durbayn	Followed Adamnan as abbot of Iona
Duach	Duke	A king of ancient Munster
Dualtach	Dooltok	"Black jointed"
Dubtach	Doovtok	A court poet in Saint Patrick's time
Dungall	Doongall	An astronomer at Bangor University

E

Eachann	Hekkan	"Horse-lord," Anglicized "Hector"
Elatha	Aylaha	A chief of the Fomorians, q.v.
Elim	Eylim	A king of ancient Ulster
Eliph	Elliv	A third century Irish prince who was martyred at Aoul in France
Enda	Enda	A sixth century saint who founded a monastery in Aran
Eochaid	Yokee	Firbolg king at Tara, early Milesian settler of Ireland
Eoin	Owen	John

Gaelic Masculine Names

Gaelic	Phonetic	
	F	
Fairceirtne	Farkarthna	A celebrated ancient poet-philosopher
Faolan	Faylan	Wolf
Feidlimid	Faylimee	A son of Tuathail, q.v.
Feradach	Faradak	A king of ancient Ireland; his mother was Baine
Feardorcha	Farry	Dark-complexioned
Fergus	Fergus	Ard Rhi, or high king of all Ireland for one year
Fethgno	Feethguno	A fourth century Irish monk who became the first bishop of Toul, Lorraine, France
Fiacha	Feeaka	A king; "Fiacha of the White Cows"
Finian	Feenian	Sixth century; master of school at Clonard
Fintan	Feentawn	Ninth century; fifty-five of this name appear in the Irish calendar of saints
Fionn	Fyon	Third century leader of the Finians; also known as Finn Mac Cool
Fionnbharr	Finbarr	Patron saint of the diocese of Cork
Flannain	Flannan	Irish saint, important in Christianizing Belgium
Foillan	Fwallon	Irish saint, important in Christianizing Belgium
Frainc	Frank	A pet form of Frank
Fricor	Freekawr	Irish saint, important in Christianizing France
Fursey	Fwursee	Famous seventh century abbot who led the Christianizing of England from his monastery

Gaelic	*Phonetic*	

G

Garbhan	Garvan	Rough; five Irish saints of the name
Gibrien	Gibrien	Irish saint, important in Christianizing France
Gilibeirt	Gilbert	"Pledge-bright"
Goll	Gull	Hero-chieftain of Connaught
Gordan	Gordon	A name among the O'Neills of Ulster
Gulban	Gulbawn	A son of Niall, q.v.
Gunifort	Goonifort	Irish saint who led the Christianizing of Germany at the time of Saint Patrick

I

Iarfhlaith	Jarlath	The patron of the diocese of Tuam
Ibair	Eebawr	A friend of Saint Patrick
Ildanach	Eeldanak	Nickname of Lugh, q.v.
Irial	Eerial	The third Milesian King of Ireland
Iosac	Isak	"May God smile"

K

Killian	Keelyan	Seventh Century saint who helped Christianize Germany

Gaelic	*Phonetic*	
	L	
Labraid	Labrawd	Grandson of Ugani, q.v.
Lachtna	Lokna	Same as Lucius among the O'Briens
Laeg	Lee	A charioteer for Cuchulain
Laegaire	Leary	A son of Ugani, q.v.
Laidcenn	Lawken	A poet at Niall's court
Laoghaire	Leary	A son of Niall, q.v.
Liam	Leeam	William
Livinzis	Liveenus	A saint and Latin poet; martyred in Flanders in 663
Lochlainn	Locklin	"Lakeland"
Longarad	Lungarad	A judge and historian
Lucan	Lukan	Name of four Irish saints
Lugadius	Lugaydius	Son of Ith
Lugh	Loo	A DeDanann chief
Lughaid	Loogaw	Early Milesian chief
	M	
Maeliosa	Mayleesa	"Servant of Jesus"
Malachi	Malakee	A warlike prince, 980 A.D.
Mannanan	Mannanan	Ancient Irish ocean-god
Maodhog	Mog	"My young one"
Mel	Mel	Fifth century abbot of Armagh
Milicho	Miliko	Saint Patrick's old master
Mochuda	Mowkooda	Abbot of Rathain
Mogh	Mawg	Opponent of "Conn of the Hundred Battles"
Morann	Morn	Law-giver; "The Just"
Muiredeach	Mwurrdak	Fourth century Ard Rhi (high king) at Tara for twenty-seven years
Muirgheas	Mawrees	"Sea-choice"
Murchard	Murkard	Son of O'Brien

91

Gaelic	*Phonetic*	
	N	
Naoisi	Neesheh	Famous in Irish legend; head of "The Sons of Usnach"
Naomhan	Nevan	"Holy One"
Nathi	Nawhi	Ancient Leinster chief
Neide	Nayda	A poet to Concobhar
Niall	Neeall	"Niall of the Nine Hostages," a grandson of Muirdeach and Ard Rhi (high king) when Saint Patrick arrived; died in A.D. 404
Nizil	Nikil	A grandson of Gaedhal
Nuada	Nooada	A king of the DeDananns
	O	
Oisin	Usheen	A great poet, son of Fionn, q.v.
Ollau	Olloo	Twenty-first Milesian Ard Rhi or high king of Eire and a famed philosopher
Oscar	Oskar	"Divine spear"
	P	
Padraig	Patrik	The national apostle of Ireland
Parthalan	Parthalan	Saint Bartholomew
Peader	Peter	Saint Peter
Piaras	Pierce	Early Norman
Pilip	Filip	Horse-lover

Gaelic	Phonetic	
	R	
Radhulbh	Ralf	Counsel-wolf
Raghnall	Reginald	"Mighty power"
Rannulbh	Randolf	Shield-wolf
Reamonn	Raymon	Counsel-protector
Redg	Rayg	A poet who taunted Cuchulain
Riocard	Rikard	"Rule hard"
Rodhlann	Rolan	Famous land
Roibeard	Robert	"Fame-bright"
Ronan	Ronan	Seal
Rory	Rory	Ancient king of all Ireland
Ruadhan	Rowan	Red
	S	
Sedulius	Saydulius	Fifth century; scholar-saint
Seganius	Sayganius	An abbot of Inis Cathaig monastery
Senach	Saynak	One of the Twelve Apostles of Erin
Seoirse	George	Husbandman
Setanta	Saytawnta	Boyhood name of Cuchulain, q.v.
Sezin	Sethan	An Irish Abbot in Brittany
Siadhal	Shiel	A bishop of Dublin
Sinell	Shinell	Fifth century; one of Saint Patrick's early converts
Solamh	Solam	Solomon
Sqeolan	Showlan	A Hound of Fionn's men
Sreng	Sweng	Greatest Firbolg warrior
Steatan	Steven	Crown or wreath
Succat	Skokat	Original name of Saint Patrick, "Clever in Way"
Suibhne	Sivney	Simon

Gaelic	*Phonetic*	
		T
Teaboid	Tibbot	Theobald "people-bold"
Theclanus	Tayklanus	An Irish abbot in Bavaria
Tiarnan	Teirnan	Lord
Tighernmas	Tee-er-nas	Seventh Milesian king of Ireland
Tiomoid	Teemord	Timothy; "honoring God"
Tomas	Tomass	Saint Thomas Didymus
Torna	Torna	A lawyer with Saint Patrick
Tuban	Toobawn	An Irish bishop in Germany
Tuathail	Tooathawl	King who established order in Ireland, son of Fiacha, q.v.
		U
Uaine	Owney	An ancient Irish name
Ugani	Oogani	Led armies into Britain, circa 200 B.C.
Uilfrid	Wilfred	"Will-peace"
Ultan	Ooltan	Seventh century; "Oolthauin," brother of Fursey, q.v.
Unfraidh	Humfrey	Peace-giant
Usnach	Oosnak	Legendary king whose famous sons fled to Alban (Scotland) in the tale of "Deirdre of the Sorrows"
		V
Vimius	Veemius	An Irish saint in Bavaria

For in the House of Tara three shadows share the feast
Conn sits in the High-King's place, against the East,
And Crionna whispers to his hound some memory of the chase,
While Connla to the harping turns a joyous listening face.

- Ethna Carbery

Bibliography

Collier, Rev., O.M.I., *Irish Without Worry for Everyone* (1942)

D'Arcy, Mary Ryan, *The Saints of Ireland* (1974)

Educational Company of Ireland, Ltd., *Learner's Irish-English Dictionary*

Hoagland, Kathleen, *One Thousand Years of Irish Poetry* (1947)

MacGeoghegan, The Abbe, *History of Ireland - Ancient and Modern* (1878)

MacManus, Seumas, *Story of the Irish Race* (1921)

O'Callahan, Maire, *Irish at Home* (1922)

O'Curry, *Tain Bo Cuailgne*

Ostrogorsky, George, *History of the Byzantine State*, Rutgers University (1857)

Proinsias Mac an Bheatha, *Irish For the People* (1966)

Stephens, James, *Deirdre*

Talbot Press, Ltd., *The Learner's English-Irish Dictionary*

Wells, H.G., *Outline of History*, Doubleday and Co. (1949)